The Flexifoil book of
Power Kiting

Navigator Guides Ltd
The Old Post Office, Swanton Novers
Melton Constable, Norfolk NR24 2AJ
postmaster@navigatorguides.com
www.navigatorguides.com

Publishers ackowledgements
Navigator Guides would like to thank all those at Flexifoil International for the enormous contribution they have made in the publication of this book. To Jeremy Pilkington for the introduction to Jeremy Boyce, an inspired choice of author. To Alan Pritchard for the design and to Andrew Jones and Mike Shaw for their technical advice. And finally to Jeremy Boyce for all his hard work and constant enthusiasm for the project.

Design concept by Alan Pritchard
Cover design by Alan Pritchard
www.baldheadmedia.com

Illustrations by Liz Johnson
Contributors: Andrew Jones and Mike Shaw
Photographers: Alan Pritchard, Andrew Jones, Carol Kohen, Christian Black, Dan Eaton, Jono Knight, John Carter, Ray Merry, Ronny Kiaulehn
Proofreading by Michelle Clark

Colour reproduction by PDQ Digital Media Solutions Ltd
Printed in Italy by Printer Trento srl

The Flexifoil book of
Power Kiting

Jeremy Boyce

Contents

Foreword

AFTER TRYING MOST extreme sports at one time or another during my life, and loving each one for whatever buzz they had to offer, I had no idea that power kiting would end up being my big passion.

Whatever direction you choose to take with kites there is something for everyone.

Flexifoil is all about the power kite and has been involved in inventing, developing and promoting power kites for over 30 years. I first got involved with Flexi in 1994, flying all their kites including the at that time brand new, later legendary, Skytiger traction foil. Flexi believed in me and my ability with power kites. With Flexifoil's support I went on to become British, European & World Champion on a kitebuggy.

In 1997 Flexifoil made a now infamous trip to Senegal, West Africa, to make a promo movie involving all aspects of the sport, to show the world what can be achieved with imagination, loads of power kite kit and 10 crazy guys. The resulting 'PowerTrip' video showed people what was really possible with kite power. However, this was just the beginning as we later went on to use the kites with mountainboards, buggies, rollerblades, body dragging, man lifting, water skiing and, finally, for kitesurfing.

This is where my life started to take a new direction: on to (mostly in to at the beginning) the water.

At this stage the Blade kite was in its infancy, being designed primarily for buggying and the high end of power kiting. Its elliptical shape, advanced profile and well balanced bridle made the Blade great for the new sport of kiteboarding as well as one of the best and best loved power kites ever produced.

The very early days of kite boarding for me had meant using the Skytiger, essentially a land-based kite but, once I jumped on the Blade I never looked back. It gave impressive lift, ridiculous power & was near impossible to collapse due to its incredible stability.

After competing internationally with the Blades since 1999, the Flexi rider and design teams realised it was lacking one major thing: relaunch from the water.

The next kite to be designed would have to be fully water relaunchable. After many ideas, prototypes and test designs, the Storm was the next break through for Flexifoil and has proved to be a huge success. Kiteboarding is the fastest growing water sport in the world right now and for sure is helping power kiting sales generally world wide.

When you think about the potential crossovers from so many other sports like, surfing, snowboarding, paragliding, skateboarding and windsurfing, the future for the power kite looks huge and when you've believed in this sport for as long as I have, it's fantastic to see the whole thing booming. I'm really excited to see what the future holds.

Jason Furness
Flexifoil sponsored rider
July 2002

◀ *Jason in action*

History

Introduction

IT HAS BEEN OVER 20 years since the development of the first steerable stunt kites. It has been over ten since the first commercially available kite buggy heralded the kite traction revolution that has brought power kiting to where it is today. We are standing on the verge of a breakthrough into the big time, courtesy of the now massively popular buggy and the new, sexy kite-god that is kiteboarding.

One company has proudly brought these milestone events to us over the years. Its name, reputation and commercial success have been built on one highly original product. It is probably the most ubiquitous kite product and name in the world today — Flexifoil.

During all that time, Flexifoil has been guilty of providing the kite industry with more entertainment and adrenaline moments, more craziness and controversy, than any other company anywhere in the world. This book briefly plots the epic tale of the rise and rise of Britain's finest and the world's best-known kite traction manufacturer — Flexifoil International.

The history of Flexifoil is the kind of story that nobody would believe could really happen if you wrote it purely from your own head. It is a story of luck, skill, chance, fate, accident, heroic endeavour, considerable peril and immense challenge and fantastic adventures.

Ultimately, the most incredible thing is that it's taken so long for Flexifoil's outstanding invention to grab the attention and achieve the popularity it now has and trigger so many spin-off activities along the way. No longer do we simply fly kites.

Like any famous invention, you could argue that someone else would have thought of it if the founders of Flexifoil hadn't, but the point is they did. It's also true that there are now dozens of designers and manufacturers of highly competitive traction kites — it's now a rapidly growing industry, such is the worldwide interest in kite-powered possibilities — and they all owe their start in life to Flexifoil. It could be said that Flexifoil has made possible the whole traction scene as we know it today.

How it all began

To get the full history, you have to make your way back through the mists of time to the mid 1970s, back to a time when there were no stunt kites, of any description.

Early days

Peter Powell, a British inventor, came up with his eponymous diamond stunter.

Around the same time, somewhere near Newcastle, two design students —Andrew Jones and Ray Merry — were experimenting with wind sculptures and facial hair. They had built a series of sky tubes of increasingly scary dimensions (although they lacked a serious lifting device for them, resorting to long poles and buildings to get them off the ground) before they embarked on their ultimate project — an inflatable aerofoil wing sculpture that could be tethered as a piece of temporary, moving public art. They even mocked up photographs of a field and, typically ambitiously, the Grand Canyon, with their creation superimposed. These clearly show, even at this early stage, the instantly recognizable profile of the Flexifoil power kite wing.

Although Andrew Jones and Ray Merry started experimenting with wind as early as 1972, it wasn't until the late 1970s, after a lengthy series of wind tunnel tests, that the first Flexifoils appeared. They were made of polythene with an externally fitted cane rod on the leading edge, but, in essence, this was the same kite that is still manufactured today as the top-selling 6' Stacker.

The beginnings of success

The two students quickly realized that they were onto something as the kites were selling as fast as they could make them (which wasn't actually all that quickly as they were still working from home and doing everything themselves). They switched to wooden ramin dowel for the leading edges and then to rip-stop nylon sailcloth before finally hitting on the fibreglass front spar that is still used in the construction of the kites to this day.

The kite's performance improved and a small workshop opened with British kite legend Jilly Pelham working on the pre-production prototypes. As one of the very early seamstresses, she helped in 'setting the standards of Flexifoil's manufacture even in those early days.'

Unable to keep up with rapidly increasing

◄ The Euro stack of 6' Flexifoils

demand, Andrew Jones and Ray Merry licensed the manufacture and distribution of their product to a new company owned by Eric Gibson. It was he who actually came up with the name Flexifoil. All appeared to be going well for 'The Flexifoil Kite Company' until, for no apparent reason, Gibson disappeared, leaving a large prepaid order for kites from a Dutch company and no kites to send it.

The Dutch connection

Desperate for Flexifoils, the Dutch customer decided to take on the manufacturing project itself. Andrew Jones and Ray Merry had not sold their invention outright and so were able to relicense the new Dutch company. Flexifoil International, as it has been known ever since, was now owned by a Dutch company with business interests in both the UK and Holland.

From the low they found themselves in at the beginning of the 1980s, Andrew Jones and Ray Merry were at a point where they were about to enjoy a period of sustained, if at first slow, progress before the final realization of their original vision.

Under its new owners, the van Dort brothers, Flexifoil International was moved briefly to Holland. It was during this period that Joost Meijerink joined the company as the General Manager and troubleshooter – a role he holds to this day.

Around this time, the bigger Flexifoils

▶ *Far right: Ray Merry and Andrew Jones*
▶ *Sky tubes: Early experiments*

began to appear –first the Super 10', then the monster Hyper 12'. These focus the impressive pull of stacks (trains of the original 6' kites linked together and flown on one set of control lines) into single kites.

Also, the Flexifoils were beginning to be attached to various objects with the idea of generating other forms of lift or some kind of traction. They, Andrew Jones and Ray Merry had already toyed around with some crude home-made buggies. Soon would come the kite-powered sailing boat – a heaving stack of Super 10's, known as Jacob's Ladder, pulling it along. Both these ideas were significant pointers to a direction that would bring future success.

Much, much stranger was the model aeroplane toy with a Flexifoil wing that hit the early 1980s modeller market – the unfortunately named WindBag. For some strange

reason it failed to capture the public imagination and it would be fully ten years before scooting along on a kart, carving up the surf and moonwalking in huge kite jumps down the beach would bring those early lift and traction efforts to a workable and, crucially, saleable conclusion.

A parting of the ways

In the mid 1980s, Ray Merry left Europe for America to set up Cobra Kites. Flexifoil still retains a design and distribution exchange relationship with the company. Indeed, Cobra has been responsible for subsequent major mutual commercial successes with the Scorpion delta wing sport kite and, more recently, the big-selling Skytiger traction foils.

Back to the UK

For reasons personal to the van Dorts, Flexifoil International moved back to Britain in 1989, to Newmarket, in Cambridgeshire.

As the kite industry generally, and rather appropriately, took off in the mid and late 1980s, Flexifoil soon established itself as the major player in the market. Its kites were top of the shopping lists of numerous new kite shops that were opening up at that time.

From then until now

The rest, as they say, is history. As the 1980s turned into the 1990s, Flexifoil continued to

▸ *Right: An early Flexifoil Stacker 6*
▸ *Far right: An awesome stack of Hyper 12's*

be — and still is — among the market leaders in terms of product development and promotion. One eye is constantly cast on the need for progress and innovation, the other on protecting what it's already got.

Always, new products and refinements are coming through that reflect — or, more often, anticipate — shifts in the market. Everything is carefully protected by series patents, continuously updated to reflect the company's meticulous approach to design innovation and improvements. Only recently has Flexifoil allowed some supplementary production to start up away from its present

factory unit in Soham, to which it moved in the early 1990s. Moving production from under its watchful gaze to a remote location abroad has had to be done to cope with the extraordinary demand for its kites.

Flexifoil has, for a long time, led the kite industry in professionally promoting and advertising its products, keenly aware that, as far as persuading punters to part with their money is concerned, seeing is believing. This explains events such as the 1999 kiteboard Channel crossing and the legendary Le Touquet 208 stack. At Le Touquet, a single stack of 208 6' Flexifoils was anchored to

two giant bulldozers on this Normandy beach. It also explains the fact that, over the years, the company has published a series of high-quality, colour, glossy catalogues and promotion materials as good as anything you'll find on the high street. In fact, 'street' is exactly where its latest club-style graphics and radical videos are taking the company and exactly where its immediate future lies.

Flexifoil's Battlebus trade show stand, complete with video wall, demo products and knowledgeable, enthusiastic staff, has prob-

▲ *Yachtsman Ian Day on Jacobs Ladder powered by Flexifoils*

▲ *Above right: The windbag*

ably done more to sell kites of all descriptions than any other single thing in the industry. That is, except for the ground-breaking (for the kite industry) series of promotion videos, each progressively more daring and challenging, slowly bringing us to the present day with all the latest kiteboard, buggy and jumping stuff, complete with techno soundtrack, helping it sit easily alongside the snowboarding, windsurfing, paragliding and other such videos at your local extreme sports shop. The outstanding in-store product display and video stand can now be found in many of the hundreds of Blacks (Camping), Free Spirit, Air and Milletts shops, as well as other radical sports shops in

the UK and the signs are that there's almost no limit to how far the company can go.

The future is bright

Having led the kite market as fast and far as it can go, the new Flexifoil objective has been to take its products out to the markets that seem most compatible with them. That's why there's such a big effort going into the surf side, with instructors and surf shop owners (who are stocking kites and other kiteboarding equipment in a big way) rapidly being inducted into the dos and don'ts of power kiting before getting into the serious stuff out on the water. That's also why the company has employed Jason Furness — presently one of Britain's leading kiteboarders (not to mention his being placed sixth at the 1999 World Championships in Hawaii) — as its demonstrator, instructor and stunt-puller-in-chief as far as that side of the business is concerned. That's also why Flexifoil was happy to organize its 'controversial' cross Channel stunt, irritating French kiteboarders and immigration officials but nevertheless gaining far more in its traditional target areas of exposure and notoriety. The roster of sponsored riders/promoters includes Chris Calthrop, Danny Seales and Andreya Wharry — all Brits of course — as well as the American rider Peter Trow.

Sitting quietly at his computer at Flexi's industrial unit headquarters, taking it all in, you'll normally find the same Andrew Jones (less hair, better trousers). He is still the designer (the recent highly successful Blade traction foil is one of his) and tinkerer-in-chief, as well as coordinator of workshop production, sourcing and getting materials when they're needed.

Until very recently, at the next desk — when he wasn't off somewhere filming himself or someone else doing something unspeakable with a kite — was the other half of the Flexi design team, the unmistakable, dreadlocked Andy Preston. He has been the master pilot in all disciplines, mastermind behind the Stranger, Psycho, Matrix and Erazor sport kites, as well as a significant contributor to the design of the Blade and Nexus traction wings.

Like Flexifoil itself, Andy Preston took a while

World record stack of 208 Flexifoils 1993

longer than he expected to really make his mark in the kite industry. However, having safely achieved his aim, he's been like a kid in a toy shop, running loose in the Flexifoil factory, constantly tweaking and resewing kites, testing, tweaking again, testing again, and so on and so on. Between them, Andrew Jones — never happier than when he's out test flying — and Andy Preston have given Flexifoil its edge in product development.

The recent addition of Jeremy Pilkington — the hard-working sales and marketing guy —

to the company's ranks has already started to pay dividends. Flexifoil recently won two prestigious business awards for the quality of the packaging and its retail, wholesale and distribution and, certainly, there is a professional cutting edge to the craziness these days. There's absolutely no doubt, Flexifoil is ready for the new millennium, poised to exploit the huge growth that seems certain to follow in power and traction kiting.

Being first in a market is a great advantage,

but you've still got to make it work. Success in the kiteboard market could carry the company to a new level altogether, but the competitive nature of it means that the water relaunchable kite may be vitally important to that future success. A fully water launchable wing is vitally important to future success. Flexifoil have successfully developed and launched the Storm to fill that gap and rightly are optimistic about the future. The stakes are high, but the possibilities are limitless. Wherever they end up, as Andrew Jones himself says, 'It's just great to use the wind to go somewhere.'

▶ *Top: Channel crossing 1999*

Team rider Jason Furness

Team rider Danny Seales

Team rider Andreya Wharry

Team rider Chris Calthrop

Team rider Aaron Hadlow

Team rider Peter Trow

Basics

"I've jumped out of planes and everything but for me the buzz you can get from power kites stands on its own – something you have to have a lot of respect for, but with big rewards for sure."

Jason Furness
Flexifoil–sponsored kiteboarder
and demonstrator

One line good, more lines better

ESSENTIALLY, THERE COULDN'T be anything much more basic than flying a two- or four-line stunt or power kite. Think bike riding without the complication of pedalling to keep moving.

To control the kite, you move the control bar push-me-pull-you style, pulling right to turn right, left to turn left, hands parallel to go straight. Good kites (or 'wings' as the kiteboarders call them) come with instructions, but there are all kinds of little dos and don'ts that you pick up with experience that help build your comprehension of how the wind and the kites work together to deliver the result you're looking for — endless hours of fun and amusement. You may learn simply for pleasure of flying the kites or it might all come together one day so you can save your own or someone else's life. No amount of instruction books and videos can make you into the perfect pilot because, ultimately, there's no substitute for getting out there and flying.

Once you get a two-string power kite flying, you can completely control it and manoeuvre it exactly where you want it to go. The kite will want to move forwards almost all the time and it's up to your piloting skill to keep it moving around without crashing into the ground or into any other kites. You also have to work at making sure that the flying lines never get so twisted by repeatedly turning in one direction that you lose all response from the kite. This might sound complicated, but it actually requires less mental and physical agility than many everyday activities, such as using a mobile phone or driving a car.

That is not all as there is also a whole generation of manoeuvrable traction kites out there with not just two but four control lines. They are even more technically sophisticated, more controllable and can, in the right circumstances, be manoeuvred more precisely to deliver even more power. They have helped take power kiting to where it is today — a sport with many layers of sophistication and enjoyment that is surprisingly easy to get the hang of. This helps to explain much of the enormous popularity of power and traction kiting as an extreme sport and leisure pursuit.

◀ *Simple kite maintenance*

▶ *Traction kite guru Andy Preston flying a Stacker*

What is power kiting all about? What's the crack?

"I first got hooked on the idea in about 1988. I saw this guy flying a stack of Flexis. He lost all control, came flying past me and my brother at about mach 10, upside down, shot through the middle of a football game using the players as brakes 'til his kites hit the ground. I was on the floor crying with laughter, at the same time thinking I've gotta try that."

Jason Furness
Flexifoil-sponsored kiteboarder and tester

Clearly we would in no way condone anyone flying out of control and dangerously close to other people as this chap appears to have done. Nevertheless, the short answer to the question 'what is power kiting all about?' is, the flying of large single or stacked (several kites linked together) manoeuvrable kites in such a way as to achieve traction. 'Traction' means generally being dragged around — and often above — your chosen flying site by whatever means possible. These means can include skidding or skudding (being dragged along on your feet or back), jumping or getting airs, body surfing, buggying/karting, mountainboarding, roller-blading, boating, waterskiing, skiing and snow-boarding. Then there are always a couple of other ways that have been added to this list more recently, but, in many ways, they are now power kiting's 'market leaders' — kiteboarding and kitesurfing.

The longer, and somewhat more considered, version of this is that power kiting is all about learning how to use the elements — in this instance the wind and your physical location — in a safe and controlled manner so as to deliver the maximum enjoyment with the minimum risk.

It is important to say here that power kiting qualifies for listing as an extreme sport. This means that extreme injuries, even death, can occur (indeed, have occurred) if the proper respect and attention are not paid to what you are doing. You have to start this process with yourself, but it applies equally to your equipment and the weather conditions on the day. You need to be certain that you know what you're doing and understand your limits and your equipment's limits and potential. Whatever level you're doing this at — either for pure recreational pleasure now and then or because you want to be a star rider on the kiteboarding pro tours — you must fully understand how your kite works before you start taking risks. Of course it's accepted that the attraction of extreme sports is the risk and consequent adrenaline rush that comes with it. The trick is making the risk whether you succeed or not rather than whether you end up in hospital or not.

Successful power kiting means working out where your limits are and pushing them gradually further and further until you reach that 'buzz' that it is all about. Like many power kiters, you may find that, once hooked, you can never get enough, always

◄ *From top: Stacker, Proteam, Super 10*

▶ *Flexifoil's Danny Seales in action*

looking for more power and more danger — going faster, jumping higher and so on. That buzz comes at a price, one you should start paying straight away by reading the following safety advice.

Safety

Walk, don't run

It's vitally important so it's worth repeating until it becomes a mantra:

SAFETY IS THE RESPONSIBILITY OF THE FLYER, SAFETY IS THE RESPONSIBILITY OF THE FLYER

Just like most other extreme sports — especially if you're going to be taking it up in the air or on to fresh or sea water — you need to familiarize yourself completely with your equipment at the outset. Learn how to control a kite of manageable size properly before you start risking life and limb on any of the large number of serious traction and sport wings on the market today. Once you've mastered the basics, you'll be ready to get going with some of the big, adrenaline-inducing wings Flexifoil is synonymous with. All the same, be ready to be shocked and surprised by just how much 'grunt' these wings can generate and never underestimate what can happen when you start playing around with the elements, such as wind and water. What you take the time to learn today might well save a life tomorrow — your own or another's.

It's worth remembering that a kite is a sail, just like on a boat, and that the bigger the kite, the greater the power it can generate. The risk of personal injury is ever present, so let's just say that if you are one of those people who falls hard and breaks easily, then maybe power kiting isn't for you. If, on the other hand, you know how to fall without hurting yourself and you bounce rather than break, read on.

You will need a reasonable level of fitness if you want to really get to grips with the big power generators. If you aren't already fit, you will need to build up to the big boys by flying smaller kites to begin with. Move onwards and upwards, literally and metaphorically, in stages. Torn muscles and tendons can easily happen — injuries that take time to mend and will keep you off the flying field for lengthy periods. Broken wrists, ankles and collar bones can all too easily result from heavy landings on hard surfaces. In any event you will find, after your first couple of sessions, that power kiting works on different muscles and in a different way to any other sport you might be used to. Expect to feel some aches and pains in unusual places as your body adjusts.

With the speed of technical innovation there has been in power kiting recently being so fast, there are now lots of pieces of equipment and safety aids available to the modern power kiter. In many cases, these are tagged on to the kites, especially in kiteboarding. Harnesses are common in kiteboarding and buggying, otherwise you couldn't cope with the huge pull of the kites for any length of time. Never, however, under any circumstances, permanently attach yourself to the kite(s). No matter how good you are, the unexpected can always happen and you may need to separate yourself from the kite quickly. Quick releases, depower systems, flotation jackets, crash helmets, knee and elbow pads, goggles and so on are all part of the power kiter's essential equipment. However, never forget that the first level of safety lies with flyers themselves. Honesty and awareness regarding your own skill level and experience, understanding your equipment and the conditions on the day — these things can save you an immense amount of trouble and injury.

Whatever equipment you've got, you'll need to check it over frequently for wear and tear. Equipment failure at an inopportune moment — especially out on the water and/or up in the air — could have serious consequences. Take or send equipment back to your dealer or the manufacturer. Many kites and other pieces of equipment are guaranteed against faulty manufacture or unexplained failure. That's not an invitation to trash your kite to bits and expect it to be repaired or replaced free of charge. There are clauses about 'normal wear and tear' in all guarantees and retailers and manufacturers are eagle-eyed — they can spot mistreatment a mile off. Look after your equipment and it will look after you, getting any repairs required done without delay. In any event,

◀ *High-speed buggy wipeout*

money spent on a repair could be a lifesaver and you can't put a price on that.

Safety is more than just a personal issue. A little carelessness or overenthusiasm can mean crashing your kite in to or on to spectators and passers-by. While many power kites are, in principle, soft (there are no rigid frame parts), they can, as mentioned, generate enormous power and it is this that causes serious injury. It's not just the kite, though, that can be dangerous. Between you and the kite can be anything up to 45 metres (49 yards) of flying lines moving through the air under extreme tension. The flying lines are thin and made from high-quality, lightweight materials to reduce drag and make the kites more efficient. This is a potentially fatal combination as the end result is that the lines have a cutting capability similar to cheese wire. There are stories of careless power kiters losing fingertips or severing ears with their flying lines. Take care and always disable your kite and flying lines on the ground when you are not using them.

It is your responsibility as a flyer to make sure you have adequate space for what you are doing. You must allow a clear space downwind of where you're standing that is at least twice the length of your flying lines to allow for being pulled forwards, especially during the launch phase, and a similar amount of space to each side. If people come too close or stand under the kite(s) while you're flying, you must fly your kite to a safe place (above your head or landed) and either

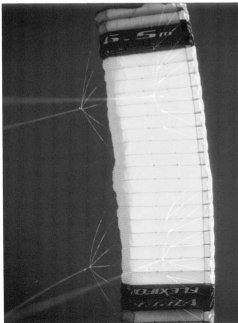

◀ *From top Viper 2m, Viper 6.5m*

▶ *A harness*

ask them to move or move yourself until it's safe to fly again. You might want to think about some kind of public indemnity or liability insurance. Many clubs and associations offer this as part of their membership and it is recommended that you take out appropriate cover.

There are some other 'contraindications' for kiting. The kites and flying lines provide an excellent earth for lightning, so at the first flash of lightning or, better still, dark cloud or rumble of thunder, get your kite down as fast as possible. Equally, a kite that dumps itself in electricity lines will not only fry itself and possibly the flyer, it will quite conceivably short out a part of the National Grid and land you with a hefty fine from the electricity company. It goes without saying that sites next to roads and railways are a complete no-no and anywhere near an airport is usually prohibited.

All Flexifoil power kites come with full operating instructions and a safety warning notice. Read them well before you take your kite out for the first time. There are some specific safety rules that apply to kiteboarding, buggying and the more extreme activities that we'll cover in later chapters, but opposite there is a general summary of what you need to do to keep yourself and others safe.

One final thought on safety before you launch your power kiting career. With the exception of when you're using kites for getting airs, when it's recommended that you hang on to the controls at all times, your ultimate safety mechanism is to let go completely of the control handles or bar if you feel that it's all getting too much. This really is a last resort, of course, and all other efforts should be made to control the kites first. This is because letting go presents a potential danger to other kiters or bystanders and means that there is a lot of sorting out of lines and kites to do before you can fly again. Never attempt to stop an escaped kite by grabbing the flying line — it may cut into your hand. In kiteboarding, where the biggest power is generated by the kites, safety systems and leashes are now commonplace so that you can let the kite go and recover it again without any kind of risk.

▸ *Blade safety depower system*

Wind speeds

If you're just starting out with power kites or are just in it for a bit of recreational fun, a basic understanding of wind speeds may well be enough. There's either enough wind to fly or not, and if there's enough, is there just enough to fly or is it strong enough to make it good fun? It's a popular misconception of our time that you need a roof-lifting wind to fly kites. Normally, most kites will fly well in 10 mph or more wind.

If you're getting a bit more specialized and enthusiastic, so you're power kiting and want to get in your buggy or out on your board as often as possible, then a little more detail will be needed. For instance, you'll almost certainly have more than one size of kite depending on what the wind strength is. In a light wind, you will need to fly a big kite (a 9.0 m Blade II, for example) to achieve traction. However, the same kite in a big wind will be an uncontrollable monster and so you'll need less kite to achieve the same power — a 2, 3 or 4 m. It's the same principle as sailing and windsurfing. The more serious you get, the more kites you'll have so that you can always max your fun, whatever the wind.

All kites come with recommended wind ranges for optimum performance, which you should treat with the utmost respect. This is very important as flying outside those wind ranges might cause damage to your kite or yourself. A set of kites with overlapping wind ranges will cover you for every eventuality.

Kite wind ranges are normally expressed in wind speeds. There are quite a few different ways of measuring speed:

- Beaufort — force 1 ,2, 3 and so on — as on the shipping forecast
- miles per hour
- kilometres per hour
- knots
- metres per second

Understanding these and what is the right range for your kite is one thing; actually measuring it on the day you're out flying is another thing altogether. There are a few ways of doing this.

First, watch the weather forecast on television. This will usually give forecasted wind speeds (in mph in the UK) in a circle on the chart, with a little arrow attached to show their direction.

A better and more accurate way is to buy yourself a pocket wind meter, but you'll need

to spend a decent amount of money to get something that is at all accurate. If you're sailing from a centre or club, it normally has a high-quality anemometer on site, giving a constant, accurate reading.

A less scientific, but nonetheless useful, method is to look for wind indicators in the environment that can give you an enormous amount of information. Watch for smoke or clouds in the sky, flags and trees moving, look at the surface of water for rippling, white horses, waves and so on. Study the table on page 23, which shows all the official measures and a list of indicators you can use.

With time, you'll learn to 'feel' the wind and make your decision on which kite to use based on your experience. You'll know instinctively when to switch to a smaller or bigger kite from your muscle and brain memories of similar situations. One thing you do need to understand is that there's a point at which kiting becomes dangerous however you're doing it. Watch what the serious flyers and riders do. When it gets too big, they stay indoors. As a rough guide, anything over force 6, which is 30 mph, is going to start making things very exciting to the point of danger and foolhardiness. Over force 8, or 40 mph, and you've only got yourself to blame.

There are some other factors to consider as well. Your flying lines can make a big difference to how the kite performs in different wind speeds. It's all a question of weight, diameter, stretch and the kind of activity you're doing and the drag that results from that combination of factors. Modern power kite flying lines are made of materials that minimize all three factors, but you may still be able to 'tweak' extra mph of wind range out of your kite by flying on lighter or heavier lines — lighter to generate more power and fly faster, heavier to fly slower and 'brake' the kite. The instructions for Flexifoil power kites suggest which flying lines have the appropriate strength for average and heavy use.

The final thing to take account of is wind direction. It may be a crucial factor if you're a kiteboarder as an offshore wind — that is, a wind that is blowing out to sea — can result in you being blown towards the dangers of the open sea and make it very hard to get back. The main thing to consider, though, is the smoothness of the wind. Beach sites are great because, often, with an onshore (blowing from the sea) or side wind,

it is smooth and controlling the kite is much easier because it behaves consistently in such conditions. An offshore wind will have to come across the land mass and any other obstacles behind. This will make it what kiters call 'lumpy'. A lumpy, gusty wind will make the kite fly erratically and, depending on its size, dangerously. Many inland sites have lumpy wind for exactly this reason. To give you a guide, it usually takes the wind up to seven times the height of the obstacle in lateral distance to smooth itself out again (ergo a 30.48-metre/100-foot tree or build-

ing will have a wind 'shadow' up to 213.3 metres/700 feet long). Clearly, you need to find the most open, exposed site you can and position yourself as far downwind of any obstacles as possible.

▲ *Left: 9m Blade*

▲ *Right: A wind meter — a very useful gadget*

The wind table

| | Wind Speed | | | | | Wind Speed Indicators (probable) | |
Force	MPH	Knots	KPH	Metres/sec	Description	At Sea	On Land
0	<1	<1	<1	0-0.2	Calm	Smooth as glass	Calm; smoke rises vertically
1	1-3	1-3	1-5	0.3-1.5	Light Air	Ripples with no appearance of scales; no foam crests	Smoke drift indicates wind direction; vanes do not move
2	4-7	4-6	6-11	1.6-3.3	Light Breeze	Small wavelets; crests of glassy appearance	Wind felt on face; leaves rustle; vanes begin to move
3	8-12	7-10	12-19	3.4-5.4	Gentle Wind	Large wavelets; crests begin to break, scattered whitecaps	Leaves and small twigs in motion; light flags extended
4	13-18	11-16	20-29	5.5-7.9	Moderate Wind	1-4ft waves; numerous whitecaps	Leaves and loose paper raised up; flags flap; small branches move
5	19-24	17-21	30-38	8.0-10.7	Fresh Wind	4-8ft waves; many whitecaps; some spray	Small trees begin to sway; flags flap and ripple
6	25-31	22-27	39-50	10.8-13.8	Strong Wind	8-13ft waves forming whitecaps everywhere; more spray	Large branches in motion; whistling heard in wires
7	32-38	28-33	51-61	13.9-17.1	Near Gale	13-20ft waves; white foam blown in streaks	Whole trees in motion; resistance felt in walking against wind
8	39-46	34-40	62-74	17.2-20.7	Gale	13-20ft waves; edges of crests beginning to break; foam in streaks	Whole trees in motion; resistance felt in walking against wind (again)
9	47-54	41-47	75-86	20.8-24.4	Strong Gale	20ft waves; sea begins to roll; dense streaks of foam	Slight structural damage occurs; shingles blow from roofs
10	55-63	48-55	87-101	24.5-28.4	Storm	20-30ft waves; white churning sea; rolling is heavy; reduced visibility	Trees broken/uprooted; considerable structural damage occurs

The wind window

Anyone who's come to power kiting from another wind sport might be more familiar with the term 'wind envelope'. It's the actual area of sky in which you can control your kite's manoeuvres as it flies at the end of its lines with the flyer standing still. The size of the wind window dictates how much and what type of power your wing will generate. Try it for yourself and you'll feel that there's a limit to each side of you and how far over your head that you can fly the kite before it either stops moving and/or loses power, stalls and falls out of the sky.

With you as a fixed point at its centre, the wind window described by the kite resembles the surface of a quarter of a sphere. There really isn't any kite that can make the full quarter sphere as this requires a full 180-degree lateral pass — it is more like 130 to 140 on average. The illustration on page 25 show how this works.

Bear in mind, too, that the wind — especially a light wind — can shift and change direction. Your orientation also shifts with the wind until you locate the centre and edges of a new window. On a beach site, wind shift could well be associated with the tides. For example, a flat calm day can easily turn into a real hoolie following a tide change.

Traditionally, sport and power kites are most efficient when they are flying at the centre of the wind window and horizontally across the sky at roughly head height or slightly above. Here they move fastest and pull hardest. Keep flying horizontally and the kite will gradually slow down and lose power as it reaches the edge of its window. Turn the kite round just before the edge and fly it back across the wind window. As you reach the centre, turn it upwards and fly the kite straight up the wind window. If the wind is strong enough, you'll notice yourself being pulled by a rush of power, followed by the same slowing down and depowering effect until the kite reaches a 'parked' position up above your head. This is known as the zenith or 'safety' position. There's almost no power in the kite up here and it's the place to try and steer the kite if you ever feel you're getting into difficulties.

Flying a big power kite near the centre of the window will generate enormous lateral pull and this is where you'll find yourself leaning right back, even lying down, to stop yourself being pulled over and dragged along on your front. In fact, you rarely see buggy drivers or kiteboarders fly their big kites near the centre of a window because the lateral pull would be too much to hold, leading to a big horizontal wipeout. What they do is use a different part of the window to generate the kind of power that is most useful to them. As with wind speeds, it is something that is worth understanding in principle but will become much more of an intuitive thing with experience. Your skill as a flyer will be in learning how to manipulate the kite in the wind window to deliver the kind and quantity of pull you want. Generally speaking, lighter wind means a smaller (narrower and lower) wind window in which the kite will be moving relatively slowly. You'll need to really work it near the edges and even at the centre to achieve real power. In a big wind you'll find that the kite flies quite differently — it has a bigger wind window, is much faster (not least because smaller kites always fly faster) and has a strong pull over a much bigger area of the window than it does in a lighter wind.

▲ Kite in the neutral position

The wind window

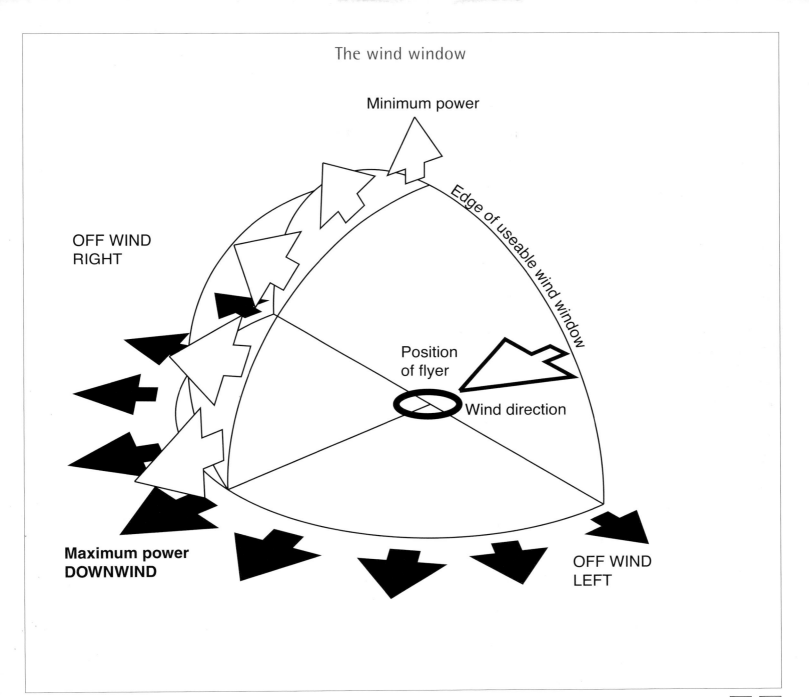

Minimum power

Edge of useable wind window

OFF WIND RIGHT

Position of flyer

Wind direction

Maximum power DOWNWIND

OFF WIND LEFT

Two Line
Power Kites
for land use

"These are great starter or recreational kites on which you can learn the basic skills and add to them. They're a sociable kite because friends can join kites together for a bigger pull."

Andreya Wharry
Professional kiteboarder and power kite instructor

The Flexifoil Stacker 6', Proteam 8' and Super 10' and recreational flying

You could say that anyone who's not a pro board rider or buggy driver is a recreational flyer. Many are just out for the pure fun of it, not too worried about developing their flying skills and not too concerned about getting on to a board or in to a buggy. If you're the kind of person who likes to keep your kites in the car to use occasionally when there's a good wind blowing, you're a recreational flyer. If, on the other hand, you like to get out as often as possible with the biggest rig possible that's appropriate for the conditions, with the added spice of big jumps, fast buggying or carving up the surf, then you're an altogether different animal.

Most people who try power kiting for the first time or start to fly regularly do start with a Flexifoil power kite. For many people the first step is going out with a friend who's already converted to kite power and having a go with theirs. The second step normally comes the day afterwards when you hunt down your nearest power kite dealer (there's a list of recommended Flexifoil dealers available at www.flexifoil.com) and buy yourself one because, like 99.9 per cent of first-timers, you're an instant convert.

If your ultimate aim is to take power kiting to its limits, then it's perfectly possible to

▸ *A stack of powered-up Proteam 8's*

◂ *A stack of 6' Stackers*

learn kite skills on one of the big traction wings. However, you can learn more, much more quickly, if you start with one of the fantastic sky-sweeping two-line Flexifoil kites. On its 40-metre (about 44-yard) lines it really fills up the sky, moving fast and pulling hard, and few other kites are able to describe the shape and extent of the wind window as well as a Flexi. Its distinctive shape has made it a household name among kite flyers the world over. Instantly recognizable individually or in the big stacks serious Flexi freaks love so much, it is the face that launched a thousand crazy power kiting pastimes.

The 6' Stacker was Flexifoil's first ever design and its enduring popularity speaks volumes for what a great invention it is. How many other extreme sports products can make the same claim that, relatively unchanged from the original concept, they've been best sellers for more than 25 years? What makes the Stacker so great is that it's easy to fly, fast, almost unbreakable and gives you a taste of what real kite power

can feel like without it ever getting too much. It's even the choice of top clergy. The late and very reverend John Habgood, former archbishop of York, having been a well-publicized Flexifoil fanatic, evidently used his for some sinfully good sessions.

When you're ready, you can switch to the slower-moving, but heavier-pulling, bigger kites — the 8' or 10' 'grunt' versions. The increase in pull through the wingspans is impressive and, with a Super 10' flying in 15 mph of good steady wind, you'll be getting one of the best workouts you've had in ages.

The Proteam 8' is the compromise kite. Fast through the air like a small kite, it has plenty of pull to exercise your muscles. Even if you do progress to far more serious power kiting extremes, you'll still keep your old Flexis in your kite bag because, for pure fun and recreational flying, little can beat these first three members of the Flexifoil family.

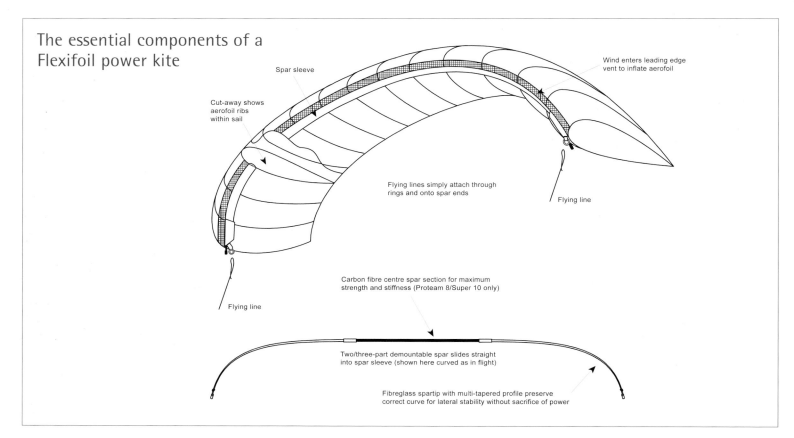

The essential components of a Flexifoil power kite

Spar sleeve

Cut-away shows aerofoil ribs within sail

Wind enters leading edge vent to inflate aerofoil

Flying lines simply attach through rings and onto spar ends

Flying line

Flying line

Carbon fibre centre spar section for maximum strength and stiffness (Proteam 8/Super 10 only)

Two/three-part demountable spar slides straight into spar sleeve (shown here curved as in flight)

Fibreglass spartip with multi-tapered profile preserve correct curve for lateral stability without sacrifice of power

Descriptions and uses

"Simplicity has helped it remain a popular recreational power kite, but its efficiency and reliability, like all functioning designs, depends on a combination of good conception, suitable materials and quality workmanship."

Andrew Jones
Flexifoil co-designer

Time to get technical again and take a close look at the basic Flexifoil kite wings and what makes them tick.

The Flexifoil Stacker was the first and original modern power kite. Although there have been changes to the materials used, its construction today is essentially the same as the original concept.

It is best described as an aerofoil kite. It's similar in basic structure to a modern rectangular parachute, or parapente. The kite is essentially two rectangular sheets of fabric that are held together lengthways, but

separated by, a series of ribs between the two to give it a three-dimensional shape. This shape is critical as it dictates the amount of lift/pull delivered. The ribs divide the kite wing into sections called cells. The kite is sealed at the rear (trailing) edge, but the front (leading) edge has a gauze opening to allow the kite to inflate, which it does under wind pressure. Once inflated, the kite has an aerofoil profile — that is, in cross-section it is similar to a conventional aeroplane wing, fat at the front edge and tapering to a point at the back. Take a look at the diagram above.

It's the difference in speed of airflow over the two surfaces of the wing, leading to corresponding differences in air pressure, that generates the power and forward movement.

Those of you who've had a look at a parachute or parapente will be familiar with the complex structure of 'shroud' lines coming from points all over the underside surface of the wing. These usually join together at two points, one on each side of the wing, and these two points are what the pilot's harness attaches to, usually hanging a little way below on two extension lines. All that string, and the need to keep it in good order, can be

▲ *Super 10' with two lines and Skytiger with four lines*

▶ *Close-up of ripstop Chikara*

a daunting prospect. However it is very necessary as these wings have no frame and require a structure of shroud lines to maintain the shape while the kite is in flight. Otherwise, it collapses in on itself, becoming a flightless piece of cloth in the sky.

Ordinarily, a soft aerofoil kite needs a similar structure and many of the big traction wings that we'll be looking at later are exactly of that kind. However, the beauty of the Flexifoil idea is its simplicity — there's very little that can go wrong. Funnily enough, the design was almost accidentally achieved — Andrew Jones and Ray Merry were unaware of other soft aerofoil wings with complex shroud lines that had already been developed. With a Flexifoil, instead of such a complex shroud — or 'bridle' in kitespeak — it has a single flexible rod that fits into a pocket that runs along the leading edge of the kite, which keeps the sail spread out in shape to fly. The rod helps the kite self-adjust its angle of attack against the wind, shifting its position on the spar in different areas of the wind window and under different levels of power. The sail tips and the control lines are attached to the tips of this rod. Once inflated, and with the tension of the control lines fixed to you, the flyer, the kite has an uncontrollable need to move forwards, and it is up to you to pilot it around the sky.

The rod itself is made of two lengths of fibreglass with a brass connecting ferrule at the centre. It has the correct combination of strength, weight and flexibility required and, as much as any other factor, the strong, stiff centre and flexible tips give the kite its classic arched shape

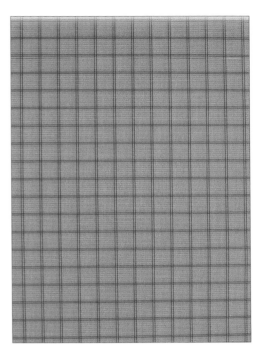

in the sky. The curve or arch of the kite is another critical factor in its functioning.

The sail material used on early prototype Stackers was plastic sheet, which wasn't really up to the job. A then new fabric was quickly identified that gave the kites the durability necessary for commercial success — one that is still in use today. Sailcloth nylon as used on yachting sails, known as 'ripstop', was the obvious choice, really, having all the qualities required to complete the Flexifoil formula, being lightweight, tough, durable and low stretch. Ripstop nylon comes in many grades or weights and, for kites, the lightest one was selected — spinnaker nylon. After a time, the demand for this fabric from the kite industry was great enough that manufacturers began to make

ripstop specifically for kites. All Flexifoil kites (6', 8' and 10') are now made from Chikara ripstop nylon, which is specifically designed for kite manufacture. The excellent colour ranges available mean that there's a good choice to enhance the look of the kites. Indeed, Flexifoil kites do look great — an important consideration when, with good wind, you're going to spend a lot of time looking at it up in the sky.

The bigger Proteam 8' and Super 10' kites use the same design and materials as the smaller ones with some modifications. Where the Stacker has 10 cells across its span, the Proteam has 14 and the Super 10' has 18. This affects something called the 'aspect ratio', which is the ratio of the depth

▲ *A young flyer enjoying his Flexifoil*

▶ *Top: Stacker 6'*

▶ *Bottom: Spar in its spar pocket*

to the span. Lower aspect ratios (the Stacker) tend to be more stable, while higher aspect ratios (the Super 10') are more efficient. The sails are also made from ripstop nylon. The front rod has the same fibreglass sections, but this time they are used as tip sections with a connecting centre rod made from solid carbon fibre. The combination of ultra-stiff carbon and flexible fibreglass give the bigger kites the same arched shape in flight as the Stacker.

Flown singly or in stacks, Flexifoils are ideal for learning how to handle power kites and can be used for taking your first steps in kite traction — body dragging, getting airs and so on. It's possible to use stacked Flexifoils for buggying, but by no means as easy as using one of the kites designed specifically for that. Although an adult toy recommended for ages 12 and upwards, children under 12 are perfectly capable of flying them — kids often learn much faster than adults. However, they will need supervision in case the kite starts to pull too much.

For sheer speed through the sky, nothing can beat a Flexifoil Stacker, and that's official. A staggering 110 mph has been clocked — a figure you're very welcome to try and surpass.

The Proteam takes you into the realms of kite traction — that is, there is enough power to start pulling a person of average build around.

The Super 10' is the undisputed best-selling power kite in the world. Awesome power, steady in flight, easy control, this is the kite to test your skill and muscles to the max.

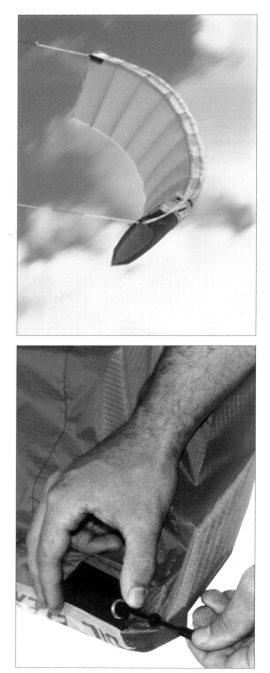

Setting up and packing up procedures

When you buy your first Flexifoil kite, it will come in its pack with a storage bag, an instruction manual, some rod/spar tape, a stacking kit and a one-month free repair card. You are thoroughly recommended to take the whole thing home, read the instruction manual, put the kite together and take it apart at least once in the calm of your living room before you head off to your nearest flying site for a blast. Standing in a windy field trying to read the manual and control the flapping nylon sail at the same time is not conducive to happy power kiting. Reading the instructions, you'll become aware of how simple these kites are to prepare for action. A quick run through confirms it. Follow the instructions and you can't really go wrong, but, if you do, take the kite back to your local dealer for some advice.

With the kite fully assembled, it's time to head back to your equipment bag for your flying/control lines and handles/wrist straps. First, take the flying lines. These are packed together on one line winder and are ready to use with a 'sleeved' loop on each end of each line.

The quality of the lines you use can make a huge difference to the efficiency, response and general flying of the kite. Nowadays, all power kite manufacturers recommend using a hi-tech flying line, such as Spectra or Dyneema, to get the best performance from

your kite. Both are synthetic fibres. Spectra was developed as part of the space exploration programme and Dyneema is a similar product. They are strong, lightweight, low diameter, have less than 5 per cent stretch and are very slippery. They enable kites to fly efficiently with minimal drag and, once 'flown in' (a few hours flying pulls any remaining stretch out), give a 'fly by wire' feel of immediate response. Conventional nylon or polyester lines are heavier, fatter and have up to 20 per cent stretch. Flexifoil-recommended line packs are always of the Dyneema or Spectra type. Their slipperiness means you can fly easily with multiple twists in the lines. Their chemical makeup gives them a low melting point, which explains the need for a Dacron sleeve at each end where the knots are tied.

▲ *Straps around a ground stake*

▶ *A Super 10*

To attach the kite:

- unwind a decent length of both lines, separate them and take one end to each kite tip
- put the looped end of line through the metal ring at the sail tip and pull a little excess line through with it
- now make a lark's head knot in the looped end, as shown opposite in the step-by-step instructions (this is the single most useful knot in power kiting, so learn it now)
- place the lark's head knot between the grommet and end cap on the spar and pull it tight
- then pull the excess line back out through the metal ring (this was only necessary to make enough room to tie the knot).

Once you've unwound the lines, you're ready for the flying straps. These are attached with the same lark's head knot as before, although it's achieved in a slightly different way:

- take the looped end of your flying line and pass it through the metal ring on the end of the straps and then pull the strap through the loop
- pull it tight and the lark's head knot will form itself around the metal ring.

The great thing about the lark's head is that it's a slip knot. The more you pull, the tighter it locks, so there's no chance of it coming undone in flight. As soon as the tension is released, after landing the kite, though, it's relatively easy to pull loose and undo.

▶ How to make a lark's head knot

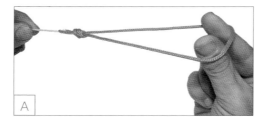

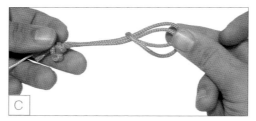

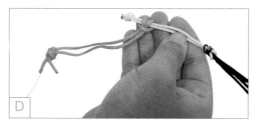

How to launch, fly and land

My advice to anyone starting out in power kiting: never ever underestimate the power of the wind and respect the elements to the full, keep the wind at your back and GO BIG!

Jason Furness
Flexifoil-sponsored kiteboarder and tester

Launching the kite

Launching can be achieved on your own or with assistance. Let's look at the assisted launch first.

- position yourself so that the kite is as directly downwind of you as possible with your flying lines attached and untwisted and the appropriate line going to each hand. Adopt a good body position — hands in the 'handlebar' position, just in front of your torso, arms slightly bent at the elbow, knees slightly flexed ready for the kite to launch and start pulling.
- your helper should hold the kite in the centre of its leading edge by the spar, which they will feel through the pocket, making sure that the kite is the right way up (gauze opening above the spar) and taking care not to block the vents with their hand. Have them hold the kite above their head and wait for it to fully inflate.
- when you're sure the kite's ready and there's enough wind, call to your helper to release the kite. They should not try to

'throw' the kite into the air — it should fly out of their hand, straight up the wind window. In lighter wind, the flyer may need to take a few steps backwards at the moment of launch to help the kite up into the air. Avoid lifting your hands and arms to encourage the kite to climb as this actually makes controlling the kite more difficult. Keep your elbows tucked in to your sides ready to start steering.

We'll look at steering in a moment, but, first, let's quickly run through solo launching.

There are two ways to do this, but both require a bit of preparation of the kite.

- the first way is to lay the kite the right way up on the ground, but at an angle, not straight on to the wind but less than perpendicular, as shown in diagram 1. When you pull the kite straight by pulling gently on the line attached to the furthest tip, it will inflate and get ready to lift off.
- the second way (which may be better than the first in very strong wind) is to lay the kite down at an angle to the wind, as diagram 2, but upside down (so the gauze is below the spar). This time you will need to make a sharp pull on the furthest tip to flip the kite over so it can inflate.

Like anything, practice makes perfect, so persevere if you don't get it straight off. Once the kite is inflated, you should follow the same procedure as for the assisted

▸ *Top: Assisted launch*
▸ *Bottom: Two solo launch techniques*

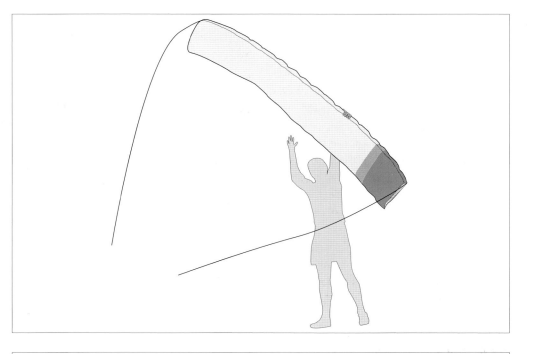

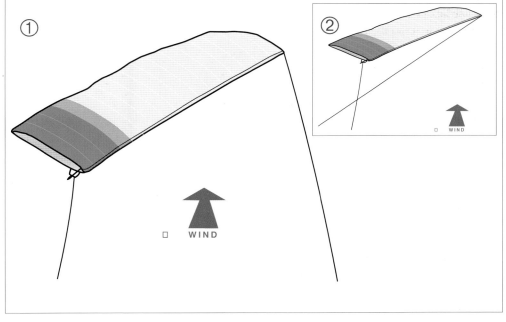

launch. Normally, the kite should lift off on its own, but you may need to help it up the first part of its journey. Don't jerk with your arms. Instead, pull back by walking steadily and smoothly backwards. Losing some ground by having to go backwards is no problem as, all being well, you're going to be pulled forwards again once the kite's flying.

If it doesn't launch fairly quickly, go and set it up and try again. Dragging the kite across the ground too much is a sure way to damage it. Use the assisted launch if needed.

Steering the kite

If you can steer a bike or a car, you can fly a power kite. The main thing is to keep your movements as smooth as possible and avoid steering jerkily.

When you launch the kite, it will fly straight up the sky (if this doesn't happen check the troubleshooting section later in this chapter). You can either wait until it reaches a hover or parked position above your head to start steering it (you'll have to watch out that you don't overfly it and drop the kite out of the sky) or, preferably, take control of it before it reaches the top of the wind window, thereby keeping it moving — the thing Flexis like best. Remember, the stronger the wind, the quicker the kite flies and the faster your reactions will need to be. Try it in a moderate wind first unless or until you're feeling really confident. Then, to manoeuvre the kite, take the following steps.

- as the kite reaches three-quarters of the way up the wind window, pull smoothly and firmly on the right line. The kite flies to the right.

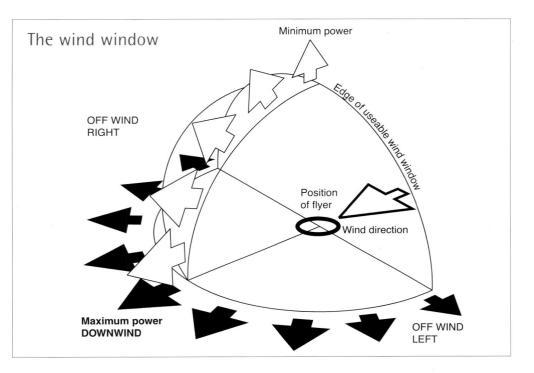

The wind window

Minimum power

Edge of useable wind window

OFF WIND RIGHT

Position of flyer

Wind direction

Maximum power DOWNWIND

OFF WIND LEFT

- pull on the left line, the kite flies to the left.
- bring both your hands towards you at the same time and the kite flies straight up the wind window.

You can spend a bit of time moving backwards and forwards across the sky like that if you like, but it's more interesting to start doing some loops.

- pull on the right line, this time keeping the pull going so that the kite flies to the right and then describes a circle downwards to the right. Don't pull the kite into a really tight spin, which tends to 'stall' the kite — a wider, smooth loop is good and is enough to bring the kite round before it

reaches the ground. A combined pull with the right and push with the left, just like on a bike, makes the smoothest turn. Keep pulling on the right line until the kite comes round and is pointing straight up the window again.

- as the kite comes round full circle and is pointing straight up the wind window, bring your hands towards you parallel with each other and it will fly straight up.

At this point, your lines are twisted round each other, but it makes almost no difference to the controls of the kite. Don't worry, to untwist the lines all you need to do is:

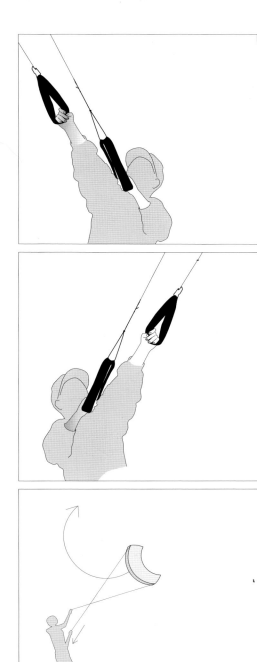

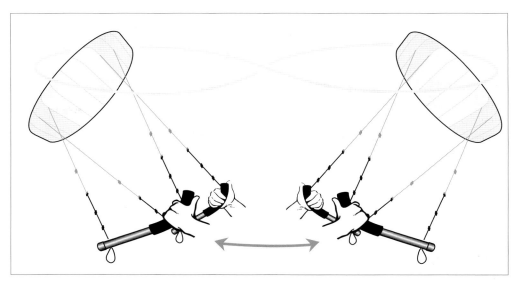

- pull on the left line hard and long enough to bring the kite round in a complete loop to the left, at the end of which, if you make your hands parallel to each other once more, should be pointing straight up the wind window, roughly in the centre
- as the kite comes up the wind window again, it's up to you, right or left, and so on.

From this point on, the freedom of the sky is yours. You can start to play with wider and tighter loops and spins, explore the wind window and get to grips with the big lateral pull low down. The best bet to begin with is to keep flying right and left loops — a figure of eight on its side — which gives you a nice continuous pattern you can fly while you

▲ Figure of eight
◄ Top: Left turn
◄ Middle: Right turn
◄ Bottom: Lines crossing/wrapping

really familiarize yourself with how the kite handles. You can fly quite a few loops in one direction before you need to untwist, but you will need to go the other way at some point. Try to keep a rough count in your head and untwist from time to time.

Flexifoils are very, very durable, which is just as well because almost certainly you'll have some big wipeouts to begin with, crashing the kites hard into the ground. It is very funny, especially when someone else does it, but try to keep your crashes to a minimum as repeated 'unintentional ground contacts' will surely damage the kite eventually.

One other manoeuvre you may want to try is a ground pass, which, with practice, you'll be able to make close to the ground.

- pull on the right line as if to do a big right loop, taking the kite down to the bottom quarter of the wind window.
- now it's all a question of timing and it may

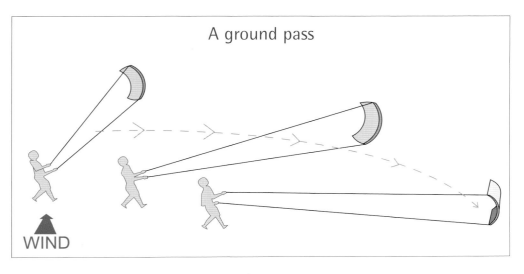

A ground pass

WIND

take a few goes to get it right. Instead of completing the loop, when the kite is pointing across the wind window, move your hands so that they are almost parallel to each other, the right hand slightly above the left, and fly the kite across the wind window from right to left.

- as the kite starts to slow down on the left side of the window, pull again on your right line until the kite is pointing across the window going back the way it came, move your hands so they are almost parallel again, but with the left above the right this time, and fly a pass back the other way.

Simply reverse the above, swapping left for right, to fly the kite in the opposite direction. Soon you'll be confident enough to try those impressive ground-skimming passes, always watching out for other flyers and stray passers-by, of course.

Landing the kite

Sooner or later you're going to get tired — especially if you're flying a Proteam or Super 10' — and will want to land the kite or pass it on to someone else. In the latter case, it's very simple. Fly your kite up to the top centre of the window — the 'park' position — slip your wrists out of the straps and pass them over to the next flyer. Even so, sooner or later, you'll still need to land. Do not fly a fully inflated and powered-up kite straight into the ground — there's a safe and simple way to do it. See page 39.

- steer the kite into a horizontal pass, as described earlier — low down if you can, but don't expect to manage this first time as it comes with practice.
- as the kite passes the centre of the window and starts flying towards the edge, keep it going in that direction.
- the kite slows down and the pull reduces

until eventually the kite flies out of the wind window and falls gently to the ground. You can take a step or two forwards to make sure it settles on the ground if you like.

The kite will normally land upside down. At this point, you should immobilize it. If it's not upside down, go and put it that way. If you're just landing for a rest, a very good idea is to use a ground stake or peg for your straps. That way, your kites can't blow away in a big gust and it will help keep your flying lines in good order. Most good kite shops sell ground stakes, but, at a push, a big tent peg will do the trick.

Congratulations, you're now an accomplished power kite flyer. Practice your controls to left and right until you're confident on both sides and you'll soon be ready to graduate to the serious stuff. That could be flying big stacks or moving on to the big traction wings for buggying and kiteboarding. Either way, you'll be joining very good company as one of the many satisfied Flexifoil kite owners.

Troubleshooting

It's worth repeating that the beauty of the Flexifoil concept is its simplicity — there's very little that can go wrong. Nevertheless, you may find that your kite doesn't seem to be flying properly. Check the following list and see how to resolve the problem.

Landing the kite

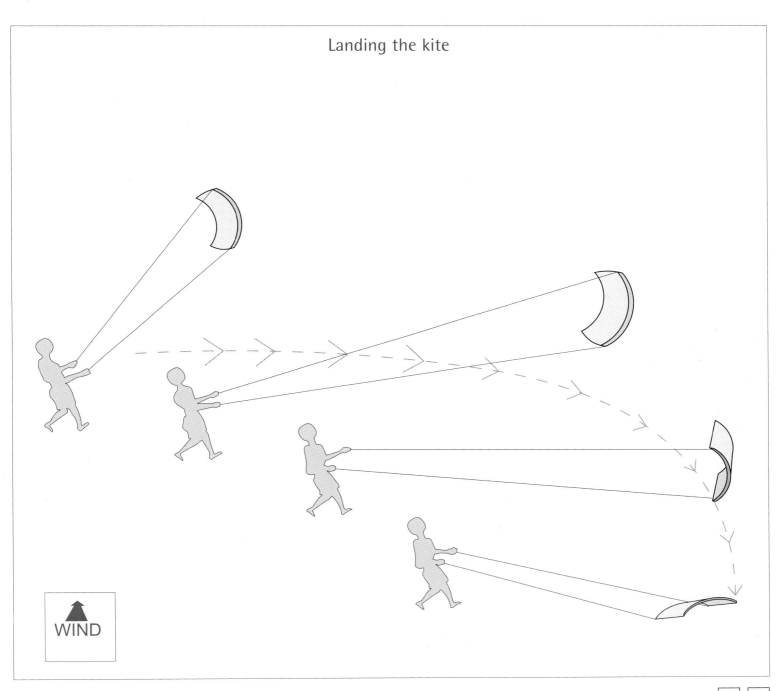

WIND

The power kite flies continually to one side

1. Check that both lines are the same length. The best way to do this is to peg the loops at one end to the ground and pull them tight from the other. A quick visual check will tell you if they're unequal, in which case you will need to make an adjustment. Undo the loop of the longest line and undo the knots holding the line sleeving in place. Slide the sleeving along until it is equal with the shorter line and retie the knots.

2. Check that you and the kite are correctly positioned in the centre of the wind window. If the kite is near the edge, it will want to fly towards the centre as soon as it launches.

The power kite 'bounces' violently in flight after launching

1. There may be sand or water inside the cells. Land the kite and try to remove the sand through the gauze vent.

2. The sail may be very wet (this problem affects smaller models mostly). Dry the sail thoroughly before relaunching.

The wingtips 'flap' during flight

1. The sail may be overstretched on the spar. Move the line attachments 1 to 4 centimetres further in. This may require moving and resticking the grommet with super glue. Flapping for long periods will eventually damage the fabric.

2. The fabric may be worn or damaged.

If the problem is anything other than the above, go straight back to your dealer or

▶ Top: Dyneema line

▶ Far Right: Damaged kite

contact Flexifoil International direct. It could be a fault with the kite, but it could also be a simple mistake you're making.

The kites are guaranteed against faulty manufacture, but not against faulty flying. Kites may well end up being damaged and Flexifoil runs an excellent and reasonably priced repair service, which you can use via your dealer or direct. Repairs to small holes can be done yourself with a repair kit. Larger tears should be sent away for repair straight away. Check your kite over regularly and ensure repairs are done quickly.

Check the spar sections, too. The carbon centre sections for the Proteam and Super 10' should not be roughly handled as they can easily chip and weaken if knocked against other spar sections.

Running without a repair is inviting bigger trouble later. You'll also have to face the fact that if you really hammer your kite, flying day in day out for long periods, especially in bright sunlight with its harmful ultraviolet rays, it (the fabric sail primarily) is going to wear out completely one day.

Stacking

'Stacking' is the term normally given to linking together and simultaneously flying two or more stunt, sport or power kites on one set of control lines. Flexifoils of different sizes can be stacked together, although it works better if the kites used are all the same size. If you do decide to stack kites of different sizes, put the smallest kite at the front (nearest the flyer) for the best performance.

There are two main reasons for wanting to stack kites, especially power kites and Flexifoils. The first is that, by adding to the first kite, you are increasing the pull on the end of your lines and, hence, the range of stuff you can do. There's a rough formula for working out by how much you increase pull, assuming you're using same-sized kites. When you add a second kite, you virtually double the pull. Adding a third adds half as much pull as the first two. A fourth will add about a third of that and so on. The point is that the pull increases to the extent that, should you decide for some reason that you want to fly a stack of 208 Stackers — as, indeed, Flexifoil did at the Le Touquet kite festival in 1993 — you'll need three bulldozers to anchor the stack and three people heaving on each line to turn it round in the sky. Get together with a few mates and you can soon have some serious traction going. You'll need friends anyway because when you're flying big stacks in a decent wind you soon get tired and you can pass the stack on to someone else.

Power kite pull is almost impossible to

▶ *A single Super 10*

quantify in terms of things like bar, especially as the wind is such a variable factor. What is relatively clear is that you can roughly gauge how the kites pull in relation to each other, even in stacks. Roughly speaking, two Stackers are equal to one Proteam, and three Stackers to one Super 10'. Two Proteams are equivalent to four Stackers, and three Proteams to two Super 10's. Three Super 10's are equivalent to a big nine stack of Stackers.

The other main reason for stacking is that it looks brilliant — to the flyer and anyone else watching. With half a dozen kites stacked, you've got a big and colourful object sweeping majestically around the sky. Looking at your kites, feeling the pull and power and knowing that you are in control is

an immensely satisfying experience, especially if you know that at any moment you could switch that power to max for some extremely radical fun. Follow the instructions for stacking kites together in your instruction manual. There are two ways suggested and either will do the trick very nicely.

You're now ready to launch. This can be done solo or assisted. For a solo launch, you should use the first method given for solo launching a single kite — laying the kites right way up at an angle to the wind and pulling them round gently with the flying lines when you're ready to launch. The kites normally inflate and lift off themselves, but you may need to take some smooth, steady steps back to get them up. As with a single kite, do not jerk with your arms.

For an assisted launch, your helper should hold the rear kite of the stack by the spar in the usual way. Once all the kites are inflated, launch as you would for one kite.

In flight, the stack should — if all your setting up and measuring is correct — 'lock' into position. If it doesn't and the kites are always 'shuffling' or simply not flying, there are a few things you can check.

- make sure all the kites are attached the right way up.
- check that the stacking lines or loops have been measured accurately.
- adjust the attachment points of a kite that seems to be lagging back, as you would for a single kite with flapping wingtips.
- try moving a problem kite to a different position in the stack or swapping its spar with another kite.

Whichever way you decide to build your stack, you will need to check your stacking lines (and, indeed, your flying lines) regularly for wear and tear. The force and friction generated is considerable. Replace any that are worn or damaged straight away.

When the stack is flying smoothly, you will immediately feel the extra power and notice that the stack flies more slowly than a single kite. The more kites you add, the more slowly it flies and the more strongly it pulls. Be aware of the strength of your flying lines. The recommended strength for a single kite will normally be sufficient for a stack of two kites the same size. Any more than that and you will need to get some stronger lines. The extra lifting power of the stack will more than compensate for any extra weight of the lines. Consult your local dealer or Flexifoil International, who will be happy to advise you. Then, you're ready for some more serious power kite action. For starters, how about a bit of skidding and getting some airs?

▲ A 4 stack of Stackers

▶ 6/8/10 Flexifoils being stacked

◀ Top: A 3 stack of Stacker 6's

◀ Bottom: Stacking off the beach

Skidding

Skidding, or skudding and body dragging, is the first way most people discover the joys of power kiting. Even if eventually you're heading for a kiteboard and the wide blue yonder, you've first got to learn how to fly kites and so you're going to learn skidding as part of your basic training. Skidding and getting airs (see the next section) require even more flying space than we've allowed before, so make sure you've got plenty of room downwind of where you're flying to allow movement forwards.

The general idea is to generate enough consistent pull from the stack to pull yourself along — usually on your feet or back. You'll be aware that if you keep flying big figures of eight with your kite(s), power is gained and lost in relation to the position of the kite(s) in the wind window. What you'll need to do to go skidding any distance is keep the kites powered up for long enough to move you along. Here's how it goes.

- steer the kites up the centre of the wind window and begin a right-hand loop. You can try it in the opposite direction by substituting left for right if you like.
- as the kites come round their loop towards the centre of the wind window, they will begin to power up in earnest. Get your feet flat on the ground and lean back to resist being pulled over on to your front. You should feel yourself starting to move forwards.
- Keep your shoulders back and your body in

a straight line, if possible, leaning back-wards, shoulders behind hips behind feet. As the kite hits the centre of the window, about halfway up, pull it into a tighter loop to keep it turning in the centre, thereby keeping it fully powered up. Too tight a spin will mean you lose power, so you may need to practice a few times to get it just right. Keep your body position and try to go with the kite, releasing the grip of your feet slightly until you're accelerating forwards.

- after a few turns, you may need to reverse the direction of the kite to untwist your lines. Keep leaning back and sliding forward on the soles of your feet.
- you can 'switch the power off' at almost any time by flying the kites upwards, out of centre of the window. Fly the kites up to the park position, stand up and walk back to your start point to have another go.

Beaches are great for skidding — hard, flat sand for speed; soft sand for really digging the feet in and 'skiing' along. Inland sites are OK, too, but you'll have a bumpier ride. From personal experience, I can thoroughly recommend a grassy playing field, recent rain and plastic waterproof trousers for one of the fastest skids you can get. Make sure you're properly kitted out wherever you're going to fly. Decent ankle-supporting footwear, a sweatshirt and comfortable trousers to prevent scratching or grazing on the ground. Even a crash helmet, wrist guards and knee pads may be necessary, depending on the conditions and the size of your stack. With practice, you'll be able to pull some amazing skids.

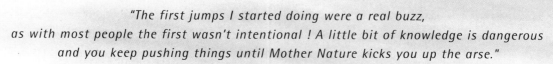

"The first jumps I started doing were a real buzz,
as with most people the first wasn't intentional ! A little bit of knowledge is dangerous
and you keep pushing things until Mother Nature kicks you up the arse."

Andreya Wharry,
Professional kiteboarder and power kite instructor

Getting airs

Otherwise known as kite jumping or moon-walking, getting airs is where power kiting really departs from normal ground-based kiting and turns into an exercise in defying gravity and achieving weightlessness. You may have seen other people getting air down at a beach or flying field or on some power kiting or extreme sport video at your local shop. You may well have experienced kite jumping inadvertently during your flying and skidding stage, but, either way, there's probably going to come a time when you want to see what it's like to get airborne kite-style.

The first thing to say is that you cannot use kites to fly in the same way that you would with a parachute or parapente, so please don't try. Nevertheless, now you really are going to have to think about some personal protection. The boots, helmets and pads are definitely necessary. There are many stories, including one about someone in England 'flying' a river estuary, of jumpers picking up a secondary gust once up in the air and ending up in a vastly different jump situation than what they'd envisaged a few seconds before. Kite jumping can be a real ankle and wrist snapper with all those heavy landings, especially in the learning phase. So, expect the unexpected and, above all, show proper respect for what you're doing. Even small jumps need big power and if things go wrong in those circumstances, you can end up in serious trouble.

◀ *A jumper with a stack of Super 10's*

▶ *Kite jumping*

It seems obvious that when jumping what you're looking for is lift rather than lateral pull. In fact, a basic maxim is to concentrate on getting altitude and the wind speed will take care of distance. This means that you mustn't bring the kites too low down in the wind window or you'll simply end up going for a facial scrape down the field. The kites must stay higher in the window than usual, which means you never use their full power. That's why you need a lot more kite up in the sky to get you airborne and that's why it becomes that bit more dangerous.

The ideal kite for getting airs will have fast acceleration to haul you up into the air and will be a two-line kite to reduce it's manoeuvrability. If you use a four-line kite, you will need to be very careful as the extra manoeuvrability and strong acceleration are harder to control because of the brakelike effect. Stacks of Flexis or single large traction kites specifically designed for jumping are the best option. Whichever you use, you will be dealing with a huge amount of kite power.

You will need to resist the kites for as long as possible until the moment of release, levering against them as the power builds up for the jump. On a beach, you can even dig a hole to give you a wall to lever against. When the moment comes and you let go for your jump, everything happens very quickly and there's a lot of energy involved — your own and the kites'. Jumping with five Super 10's in a 20 mph wind means there's about 3 Gs of force on your body as you leave the ground. You're going to need to be reasonably fit and not easily breakable. It's probably not a good idea to start off at this level.

Instead, start small and work your way up. It won't be long before you're counting the seconds of flight and making very, very long jumps. Discretion is very much the better part of valour in power kiting, however, and you shouldn't be embarrassed about stopping if conditions and the size or height of the jumps get too much.

Look at the oposite page diagrams and follow these instructions.

- steer the kite(s) up to the park position at the top centre, or zenith, of the wind window. Get ready to brace your body and find a good 'lever' position. Without pulling the kites into a full loop, steer them across and down one edge of the wind window until they're about halfway up or down the wind window, pointing slightly towards the edge. This is done with a slight pull on either the right or left line. It's common to feel more confident setting a jump up from one side rather than the other, so try both and see which feels best.
- now pull slightly with the opposite hand to point the kites in towards the centre of the window. They will accelerate and pick up power very quickly. Keep leaning back and levering them with your body. In lighter winds, you may find that running in the opposite direction to that in which the kites are moving will help crank up the power.
- as the kites approach the centre of the window, roughly halfway up, steer them so that they fly straight up the wind window. At the same time, you can release your resist-

ance to the kite and you'll feel yourself pulled, jerked off the ground, arms first, up into the sky, legs trailing behind you. Hold on tight and enjoy that weightless moment.
- watch the ground as it rushes up to meet you for touchdown and swing your feet and legs forwards, pendulum-style, so you can land on your feet or.
- once you've hit the ground again, you can recover control of the kites. They should be flying up near the top of the wind window with little pull.
- pick yourself up and, keeping the kites up at the zenith, you can go back for another jump, if you're up to it.

Make sure you're really confident before you try to hit any really big airs and it's unlikely you'll ever need an ambulance. Beaches are definitely a good bet for doing this, especially as soft sand affords a softer landing. Even so, landings can be heavy. If you do feel that it's all getting a bit too big or you pick up one of those second surges from a gust of wind, the best advice is not to let go, hang on to your wrist straps and wait for the kites to bring you down again. Take a kite or two off your stack and try again. If, on the other hand, you're in the air and heading for a large, immovable object, such as a building or tree, better to let go — it's probably the lesser of two evils.

▶ *Getting some air*

How to jump

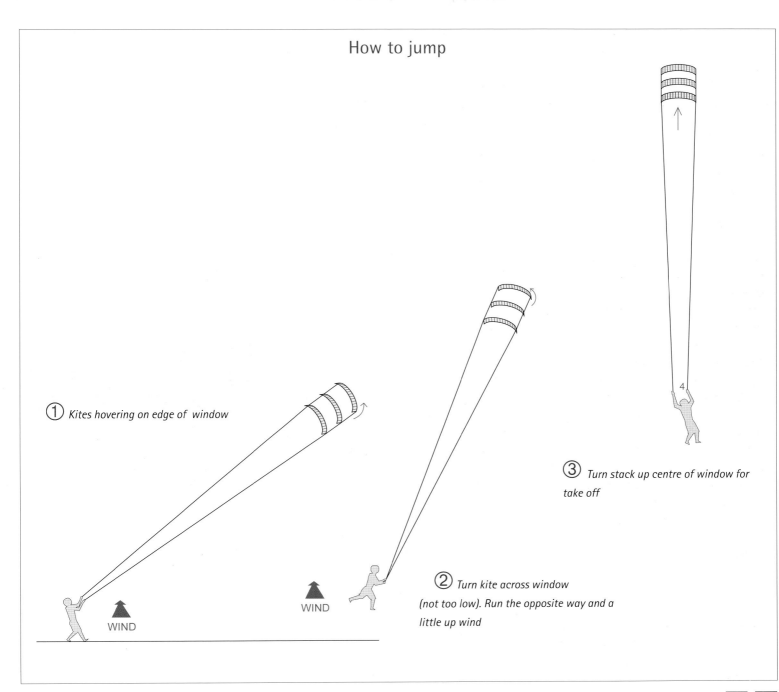

① Kites hovering on edge of window

② Turn kite across window (not too low). Run the opposite way and a little up wind

③ Turn stack up centre of window for take off

WIND

WIND

Four-line
Power Kites

"Soft four-line kites took recreational power kiting to a new level. Now you could use kites as a traction tool to propel the flyer on buggies, kiteboards, mountainboards and anything else that moves!"

Jeremy Pilkington
Sales and Marketing Manager, Flexifoil International

The four-line concept

AS THE FACE OF power kiting has changed and all manner of extra traction possibilities have been opened up by harnessing kite power to buggies, mountainboards and, of course, kiteboarding boards, so the performance requirements for power and traction kites have changed, too. The easy-to-use standard Flexifoil kite, though good enough to get you going for, say, buggying, wasn't specifically designed for the job. So, it is no surprise that the company decided to put a clean sheet of paper on the drawing board when it came to dealing with the new traction challenges that were presenting themselves.

Responding to an entirely different set of demands, Flexifoil made a giant evolutionary leap. The company started to develop soft, frameless (no spars, nor stiffeners) aerofoil traction kites, designed to meet the varied needs and usage options in the new power kiting disciplines.

The removal of the frame rod was in itself a radical enough departure for the company, bearing in mind that, up to that point, it had only ever produced the Flexifoil wings and a range of framed delta wing sport kites. There were already some soft two-line power kites available — notably the Peel, designed by Peter Lynn in New Zealand. These were generally slower moving than Flexifoils and couldn't be made in big enough sizes to deliver the necessary power for buggying and the curious buggyboat that Lynn was also manufacturing at the time. It was clear, too, from parapente and parachute design,

that this type of wing could deliver big power. However, there was to be another element to the change in format — one that has ultimately done much to facilitate the huge appeal and growth in popularity of traction kiting.

During the late 1980s, the American kite manufacturer Revolution successfully developed its synonymous and truly revolutionary carbon fibre-framed, four-line sport kite, the Revolution 1. Instead of two control lines, the new kite had four — two attached to each side of the kite sail, one at the top and one at the bottom. Special control handles were made with two attachment points on each, one handle controlling each side of the kite. Whereas a two-line kite has it's angle of attack (the angle of the sail against the wind) fixed to move the kite forwards all the time, with the new concept it is possible to engage forward movement by applying pressure to the top lines, then applying pressure to the bottom ones, thereby altering the angle of attack so that backwards becomes forwards, you can slow the kite, stop it and move it in reverse. In fact, four lines technically gives 360-degree manoeuvrability. It is the curious combination of the kite's ultra-precise manoeuvrability and its ability to stand still that catches the eye. Traction kite designers quickly saw the possibilities and adapted the principle to soft traction foils. It has been an enormous success and this innovation marks the point at which the numbers of people getting into power kites reached critical mass and the whole market became self-promoting and sustaining.

Lacking a frame, completely soft ram air

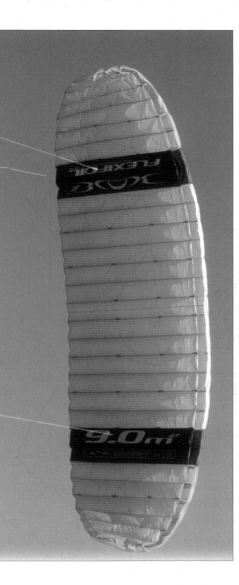

◀ A Skytiger

▲ A Blade Mark 2

kites need the multiple suspension point bridle system to hold their shape. Although this is more complex to design and not self-adjusting in flight, what it does mean is that the flyer can control the angle of attack of the kite more using the control handles and so create and use a different kind of lift. The four control lines make that control very sensitive and accurate.

As it applies to power kites, even in the four-line scenario, most of the work in terms of load bearing and steering control is effected with the front lines. The rear lines are there most of the time to help keep the kite in the right shape and for 'braking' it to reduce power. They are used much less for

▲ Left: A buggyboat conversion
▲ Right: Four-line control handles

actually going backwards. For this reason, generally speaking, the front lines are stronger than the rear ones. The control handles are each in the form of a short bar, slightly curved near the top. Top and bottom on each side of the kite connect to the corresponding top and bottom of each handle. There is a risk of attaching your flying lines upside down, so nowadays line sets are sold with colour-coded sleeved loops so you can tell at a glance which is which.

Flying and steering the kite are achieved in very much the same way as before, by pulling with your left and right hands, but the difference is that you need to keep pressure on all four lines for the kite to retain its shape. To brake the kite, you gradually apply more pressure with the rear lines until the kite slows down to a complete stop and it

will even eventually start moving slowly backwards.

The size and efficiency of these traction kites explains the increasing use of harnesses by serious power kiters. A loop of heavy line connecting the handles is hooked into the harness, which enables you to carry most of the pull on your legs and body, relieving pressure on your arms. Steering happens as normal, with the loop of line sliding through your harness hook or pulley. You shouldn't consider using a harness until you have fully mastered flying your kite ordinarily. It doesn't take long to adapt to flying with four lines, but you certainly should spend some time, as ever, familiarizing yourself with the flying controls before you get radically powered up.

There's been a long-standing misconception that kiting is an activity the potential of

which is limited by the flying line spaghetti scenario. The idea of four control lines can be even more intimidating in theory, but, in practice, everything is geared towards simplicity. Kiting has sorted out its spaghetti issues and you needn't worry. You shouldn't have problems if you are organized about how you handle your flying lines. In any event, they are a critical element of the whole kit and need to be respected as much as the kite itself. Always allow time at the end of your session to pack up in an orderly way and always immobilize your kite properly when not in use. Bad winding and a kite that blows away down the field are two common causes of fouled lines.

One major difference between Flexi and soft aerofoils is that the soft ones are very difficult to stack, requiring a different approach to the issue of having more or less power on the end of your control lines. An early idea from another UK manufacturer was a kite wing with extra sections that could be quickly zip fastened on or off. However, the idea that got the majority vote was to have a range of kites in different sizes that would enable flying in a wide range of winds. This is similar to sail boats, windsurfers and so on, which use the smallest sails in the biggest winds and vice versa. In most other respects four-line kites are the same with the same wind window and other physical limits as their predecessors.

A note of caution — just because they're soft, don't kid yourself that they cannot damage or be damaged. With no other visible means of support (a spar or frame), they are more susceptible and sensitive to nicks and tears in the fabric. Overstretching can also be a problem, especially if a kite is flown above its recommended wind range for lengthy periods. Equally, a heavy, vent down, fully inflated and powered-up landing can easily burst a panel or, worse, one of the internal ribs that are critical to the airflow and pressure within the sail. Remember, too, that, as so much power is involved, slamming the kite into a bystander could cause them serious injury. Safety is the responsibility of the flyer.

Since the development of soft aerofoil, or 'ram air', power kite wings, there's been a quantum leap in the number of power kite manufacturers who've come into the market to satisfy the increasing demand. Flexifoil has always argued that competition is good for the market, stimulating technical advances and product design, all of which can only benefit the consumer. That's certainly true in this increasingly specialized market where the last ten years have been the most productive for Flexifoil and the whole industry. Flexifoil itself has no less than three complete ranges of four-line aerofoil, or ram air, kite wings, each designed to meet a specific need of modern traction kiting.

◄ *Four-line handles – the brake position*

▲ *The harness*

Quad-line power kites – Skytiger, Viper and Blade

The Skytiger

First off the drawing board in 1995 came the Skytiger – a relatively low aspect ratio (more square than rectangular) kite by today's standards, but a cutting-edge competition winner in its heyday.

The kites have no rods or frame to stiffen them and they inflate as a result of wind pressure created by a series of vents at the front and are held in shape by a complex bridle structure with multiple suspension points, as described earlier. The extra controllability of the four-line set-up meant that the many people getting into kite buggying at that time could do so with far greater ease, allowing themselves to be pulled along and concentrating more on steering the buggy, less on piloting these super-stable four-line kites. As a result, they quickly replaced the generally faster-moving two-line foils that had been the main option up to that point.

The Skytiger was designed and developed by Andrew Jones' original partner, Ray Merry, and his new Cobra Kites venture in America. Because of their long-standing relationship, it was only natural that Flexifoil would manufacture and distribute the kite in Europe. The Skytiger has now been, for a very long time, one of the best buggy kites on the world market. Its stability makes this proven, top-level kite a superb option for the many beginners continuing to flock to the sport. Don't be fooled, though, it's no pussy-

cat – you'll still be amazed at how much these kites pull when you take the controls.

The Viper

"The Viper series traction kite is great for buggying. Its reduced lift and great apparent wind speed allow the Viper driver not to have to worry about being lifted out of his buggy."

Mike Shaw
Flexifoil's UK Sales Manager

Inevitably, design and technology overtake most great ideas and Flexifoil more recently released a new, higher-performance buggy wing for the serious – rather than the beginner or recreational – kite buggy driver.

Working with former Ford Motors air tunnel tester turned championship-winning traction foil designer and manufacturer Peter Mirkovic, Flexifoil has created another successful kite.

The new kite – the Viper – is, not surprisingly, another soft aerofoil kite with a complex bridle flown on four control lines. It, too, is a proven winner on the national buggy racing circuit. It differs from the Skytiger in having a higher aspect ratio (more rectangular than square) making it faster moving, more responsive, more aggressive and less docile than its predecessor.

The Viper is available in five different sizes,

▲ *Skytiger*

▶ *Top: Viper*

▶ *Bottom: A Viper being used for buggying*

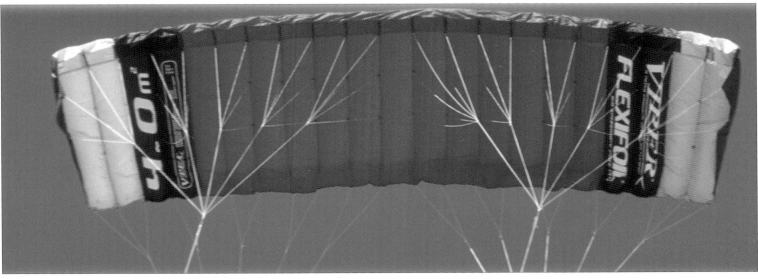

giving serious buggy drivers more options and the ability to fine tune their set-ups to deal with all the combinations of elements they are likely to encounter. It's a kite that gives an all together higher performance and requires a correspondingly greater skill level than is needed for the Skytiger in order to control it fully.

The Blade

"Nothing takes you higher faster than a Blade. It's like a rocket launcher. If you want big airs and high adrenaline, get a Blade. It's the most stable foil kite out there, making it ideal for water use".

Chris Calthrop
Flexifoil-sponsored kiteboarder

The latest twist in the power kites' tale has taken them on to the water with the successful invention and popularity of kiteboarding. Like windsurfing but using a kite for power instead of a fixed mast and sail, kiteboarding has brought it's particular set of requirements to bear on the creative forces behind modern kite design.

Flexifoil's first solution to the kite for water and/or board use is the Formula One model in its ram air foil range — the Blade. The Blade, an Andrew Jones design, is another frameless aerofoil kite with a multiple bridle and a high aspect ratio. However, this time it has a more ellipsoidal outline and rounded

◀ *At home on land or water – the Blade*
▶ *Blade Mark 1 getting big air near Dover*

wingtips — a well-proven wing form, giving a solid structure and good aerodynamic properties across the whole span.

It's a kite that develops phenomenal pull and lift to help keep the kiteboarder well up on the water. Blades were the kites used by Flexifoil's three-man team on their successful first ever Channel crossing by kiteboard in 1999. In fact, the Blade is excellent for land use, too, and is a popular choice for buggy drivers. It's available in seven different sizes, reflecting the extremes and range of conditions you need to understand when you start to play with these very serious 'toys'.

Comparing the Skytiger, Viper and Blade

A quick look at the photos on pages 56-58 will show you what the three kites look like and how much they differ from their predecessors. You can use all of them equally well out of a buggy or off the water. Of course, it's a good idea to totally familiarize yourself with every new kite wing you fly. Indeed, learning about the kites on their own first is the only way to approach the added risks of buggies and boards, so inevitably you're going to end up flying the kite as a kite at some point. You'll find that you'll be able to skid and jump as before — much more, in fact, as now the chances are you'll be flying bigger wings to suit your changing traction habits and your ever-increasing mastery of the kites and their power.

Setting up and packing up procedures

When you buy a Skytiger, Viper or Blade, it will come in a funky carry bag. Inside the bag you should find the kite, neatly folded, a pair of four-line control handles, an instruction manual and a product registration/free repair card. If any of these items is missing, contact your dealer or Flexifoil International immediately.

You are well advised to go home and take the kite out the first time in the calm comfort of your living room. There you can have a good look at it before you take the often sizeable sail out to a windy flying field, where it can all too easily turn into a flapping monster, especially when you're holding the instruction book in your teeth at the same time.

You will also need to make sure you have flying lines of the appropriate strength for your new kite.

Follow the manufacturer's instructions for setting up and packing up and you won't have a problem. In the unlikely event that you do have a problem, take the kite back to your local dealer for advice or contact Flexifoil direct (contact details are given at the end of the book). See also the care and maintenance of your equipment section of the book for other recommended storage and packing tips.

Your instruction manual also covers setting up your flying lines and attaching your control handles (or bar if you're flying the Blade on a two-line set up). You will need to be familiar with the lark's head knot to correctly attach your flying lines, so if you skipped that bit of the earlier section covering basic Flexifoil kites, it's time to go back and check it out now.

How to launch, fly and land

Launching the kite

Under normal circumstances, you should be able to solo launch.

- pick up the handles, remembering to put your ground stake in one pocket as you'll need it later to immobilize the kite and lines again.
- take one handle in each hand, holding them firmly by the foam-cushioned sections at the top, with the curves away from you and the bottoms of the handles further towards the kite than the top. The front flying line leaders should come out from between your index and second fingers and your thumbs should be on top of the tops of the handles, joystick-style. This is the 'neutral' position for normal flight.
- make a last-minute check that your lines are connected correctly — left to left and right to right, top to top and so on — and untwisted. The wind should be on your back with you and the kite in the centre of the window. The kite should still be on its back and the trailing edge weighted down.
- pull back gently and steadily with both handles, keeping equal pressure on all four lines. The front or leading edge of the kite will lift up and the kite begin to inflate with the wind pressure. As it inflates, the kite

▲ *The correct take-off position*

will stand up on its trailing edge ready to take off. You can hold it at this point until you're absolutely ready for flying.

- pull sharply on all four lines to fully inflate the kite and it will start to lift off. You may need to take a few steps back to get it moving, depending on the wind conditions. The kite will fly straight up the wind window, through the power zone, to come to a rest with minimum power in the 'park' position at the top centre, or zenith, of the window. Be ready to deal with the pull as the kite hits the power zone, leaning back with your shoulders and moving forwards a little on the ground.

Let's take a quick look at the other solo launch method and assisted launching. In

strong winds it's inadvisable to launch in the centre of the window as the kite will hit the strongest power zone of the window immediately after launch and this can be very dangerous for you and other people.

- you need to set the kite up close to the edge of the wind window in relation to where you stand, which is in line with the window's centre. Lay the kite on its back, but this time lengthways downwind so that the wind blows across the kite from tip to tip, leading edge vents facing towards the edge of the window. Weight down the upwind tip with sand or pebbles, for example, leaving the downwind tip free.
- pick up your handles and pull gently on the downwind end of the kite (the tip furthest

away), which will lift the tip and leading edge enough to allow the kite to inflate.

- keep pulling steadily with the downwind handle and the kite will launch and fly itself towards the edge of the wind window.
- keep pulling slightly on the downwind handle and steer the kite carefully up the edge of the wind window to the zenith where you can get ready for flying.

If you are going for an assisted launch, make sure your helper understands what to do.

- first of all, the helper should stand towards the edge of the window, behind the kite, holding it up so that the leading edge is facing the wind and pointing towards the edge of the wind window.
- once the kite is inflated and you're ready, call to the helper to release the kite. The helper should simply let it go rather than try to throw the kite up, which will actually prevent a smooth take-off.
- as the helper releases the kite, you fly it out of their hands, pulling slightly on the upper tip to steer the kite up the edge of the wind window to the zenith.

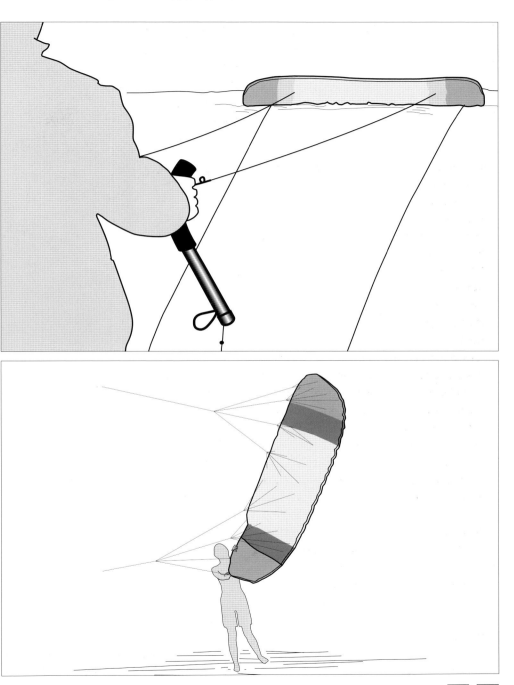

▶ Top: Solo launch

▶ Bottom: Assisted launch

Flying and steering the kite

You can hold the kite at the zenith for as long as you like, but, as soon as you're ready, you should start with some basic turns. To begin with, keep the kite high in the wind window and make gentle control movements. This will keep it out of the extreme pull of the power zone while you get used to how it's handling. The basic turn manoeuvre is similar to that used for a two-line kite.

- when the kite is climbing up the middle of the wind window and is nearing the zenith, pull back on the right handle, keeping tension on both lines. The kite turns to the right and starts making a wide, full loop in that direction.
- keep pulling on the right handle until the kite has flown a complete circle and is climbing up the wind window again, pointing straight up.
- bring your handles back to the neutral position and the kite flies straight up.
- now pull on the left handle to execute a left loop and untwist your flying lines.

You will find that as much as you pull with one handle, you push with the other because of the angle of your body and this, in fact, makes for a good smooth turn. A pull with one hand 'stalls' one side of the kite and the other speeds up around it. Pushing with the opposite one makes a similar but smoother turn by keeping the whole kite moving. You can also start to make different and even better turns by using the extra control possibilities of the two extra lines.

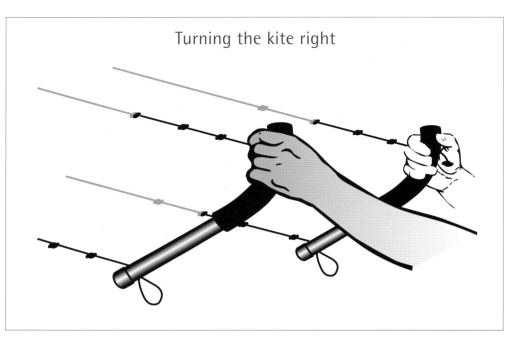

Turning the kite right

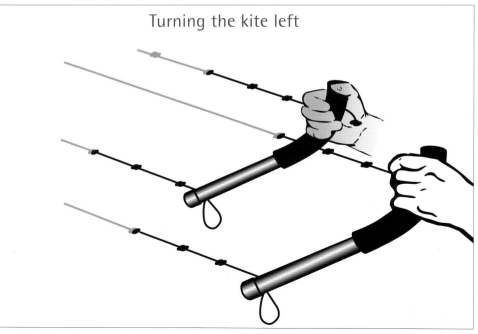

Turning the kite left

- as you begin a loop, whichever handle is being pulled should be pivoted so that the rear line is pulled as well as the top. Push your thumb away from you and point the top of the handle more towards the kite. The kite will turn faster, even spin on its axis, before resuming full power.
- as the kite comes round full circle, bring the handles back to the neutral position to resume normal flying.

As your flying become more confident, you can experiment with more power. Flying alternate left and right loops in a kind of flat figure of eight in the centre of the wind window will give the best and most consistent pull as a fixed flyer (as opposed to one moving on a board, buggy and so on) and stop the lines twisting too much.

Four-line control means having the ability to stop and reverse the kite, even depower it if needed. It requires a lot of wrist action and brings the rear lines fully into play. You stop the kite in mid air by changing the aerodynamics.

- with the kite flying up the middle of the window, leading edge pointing straight up, rotate both handles by pointing your thumbs forwards until the kite 'brakes'.
- keep pulling on the rear lines and the kite slows to a stop and starts to reverse.

- to resume normal flying, rotate the handles back to the neutral position by bringing your thumbs towards you again and pull on the front lines.

With experience, you'll be able to control the rear lines much better. Fine adjustments of your braking and 'playing' the handles a little will enable you to position and hold the kite just where you want it almost anywhere in the window.

Figure of eight

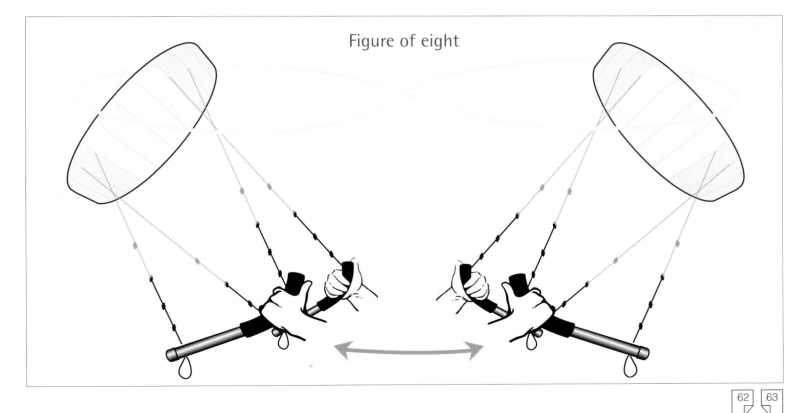

Landing the kite

Landing is an extended version of stopping and reversing the kite. Technically speaking, it can be done anywhere in the wind window as long as the leading edge is pointing up. In practice, you may find that it's easier to start by trying it nearer to the edge of the wind window where there's less power in the sail. Be careful, though – flying too close to the edge could make the kite unstable and require some juggling to keep it steady.

- with the kite pointing straight up, keeping as close to the ground as you can and your handles in the neutral position, apply almost full brakes by rotating both wrists so the tops of the handles are pointing at the kite. You should be flying on virtually the brake lines only. The kite slows and stops very quickly, depowering it.
- keep the rear lines on full. The kite will descend backwards to the ground and settle on its trailing edge. Don't try to go backwards too fast or it may flip out — that is, the bottom will come towards you. You may well need to play the handles quite a lot to keep the kite steady as it comes down the last bit before it reaches the ground.

It will take a bit of practice to get right, but, once you've landed, it's up to you whether you want to relaunch or stop flying. Relaunch as you launched first time. To immobilize the kite, peg the handles to the ground by the loops at the bottom, keeping tension on the rear lines as you do so. Then, go and weight the kite down.

▲ *The three stages of landing*

Relaunching or recovering the kite

Another advantage of four-line flying is that you can relaunch from almost any position. Generally you'll find that the kite is either on its trailing edge — in which case, relaunching is obvious — or its leading edge — that is, going forwards into the ground — making relaunching a little less obvious. However, if you can reverse the kite in the sky, it follows that you can reverse it off the ground, too. This is what's known as reverse launching.

- with the kite on the ground, fully inflated and standing on its leading edge, pull backwards (it may need you to walk backwards a few steps, too) with the rear lines only. The kite should begin to rise backwards off the ground. You will often need to 'play' the handles to keep it going steadily.
- keep pulling back on the rear lines and, as the kite rises, push one of the rear lines forwards by pivoting the handle and the kite will pivot, too. It's easier to turn the kite up and away from the centre of the window rather than down towards it as the kite will tend to accelerate towards this point and into the ground.
- when it's pointing straight up the window, you can fly away or try another landing if that's what you were doing.

If that doesn't work, there's another thing you can try. It involves turning the kite on to its trailing edge so the leading edge is pointing straight up, then you can relaunch in the normal way. This is generally easiest if you try to roll it over towards the centre of the window. If the kite is directly downwind of you, walk a few paces to one side to create a new centre, which will automatically create a new position for the kite, one that is closer to the edge of the window.

- pull back on one handle only — the one connected to the side of the kite furthest from the centre of the window — pulling, the bottom of the handle more than the top. The tip of the kite will lift up and rise until the kite is standing vertically, its leading edge pointing out of the wind window.
- at this point, you can start to bring the handle you pulled slowly back to the neutral position, still with more pressure on the bottom line. The kite should continue to roll down to a horizontal position, leading edge pointing up.
- as the kite reaches the correct position, use your rear lines to keep it still on the ground while you get ready to launch in the normal way.

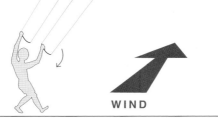

▲ Reverse landing from the edge of the window in strong winds

▶ Top: Reverse landing from the centre of the window

▶ Bottom: Reverse launching your kite

Troubleshooting

Under normal circumstances, nothing should go wrong, but, if for any reason the kite doesn't perform, there are a few things you can check.

- the bridles should not be twisted.
- the flying lines should be correctly attached — heaviest lines on the front, left lines to left handle and so on.
- you need to hold the handles in the correct hands.
- all the lines need to have stretched. Stretching can occur during your first few sessions, until the lines are fully 'flown in'. Check your lines regularly to make sure they are still all the same length. What you can do about this is explained in Chapter 8, Care of your kite and kit.
- if the kite is sluggish on take-off and slow through the sky, the chances are that your brake lines are too short and/or your main lines are too long.
- if the kite is unresponsive to steering and difficult to reverse, check if either the brake lines are too long or the main lines are too short.
- in either of the above scenarios you can make an adjustment at the handles — shortening or lengthening as appropriate — using the leader line knots.
- if the tips or trailing edge are flapping, there may be sand in the kite. Land and empty the sand out through the vents at the front.

▲ Blade's two line crossover conversion kit

If the kite still won't fly, contact your dealer or Flexifoil International direct. Expect to learn how to troubleshoot very quickly. In the meanwhile, talk to other, more experienced flyers if you can. Their advice can save you an awful lot of learning-from-your-mistakes time. After a few sessions, you'll be a fully competent power kite flyer and ready for some serious action.

Flying a Blade on a two-line set-up

There's a growing number of kiteboarders, of both water and snow varieties, who prefer the sophistication of top-range kites such as the Blade paired with the simplicity of two-line flying. Partly this is because of the use of control bars instead of independent handles, which lends itself easily to two-line flying. Partly it's because if you keep the flying simple, you can be more radical on the board. More often than not a combination of both these reasons is at the root of this combination.

Every Blade kite can be fitted with a two-line conversion 'cross over' kit, which helps speed up the turn rate of the kite. The cross over kit can be purchased separately. You'll also need to buy yourself the control bar for actually flying the kite — either a Flexifoil model or another make. Flexifoil recommends bars between 60 and 70 cm (about 24 to 28 inches) long, although it's down to your own preference in the end. A general rule of thumb for beginners is to use a longer bar with a bigger kite and vice versa. Follow the step-by-step instructions for

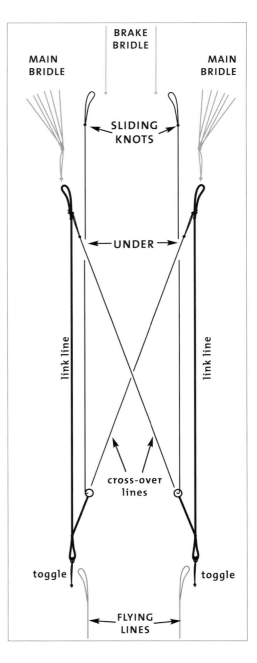

fitting the cross over kit that are included in your Blade II instruction manual. If in doubt, consult your local dealer or Flexifoil International.

Launching the kite

Whether you've used the cross over kit or not, you're now ready to attach the control bar as previously described. Make sure the lines are untwisted and get your body in position ready to launch. You can solo launch in lighter winds, but in a strong wind you must launch with a helper. In any event, you have less control over the kite with two lines and will need to set up near the edge of the window.

• lay the kite out on the ground (or have your helper hold the kite up to the wind) lengthways, downwind, with the leading edge facing the edge of the window. Weight the upwind tip down with sand, leaving the downwind tip free.

• pull on the downwind (furthest away) tip with your control bar, pulling slowly and steadily. The free tip of the kite will begin to rise and the kite will start inflating as wind enters through the vents.

• keep pulling on the furthest tip (you may need to take a couple of steps back) and, when the kite is fully inflated, it will lift off and turn itself to face upwind if you're solo launching. If you're doing an assisted launch, at this point, call to your helper to let go in the recommended manner.

• steer the kite carefully up the edge of the

▸ *Solo launching*

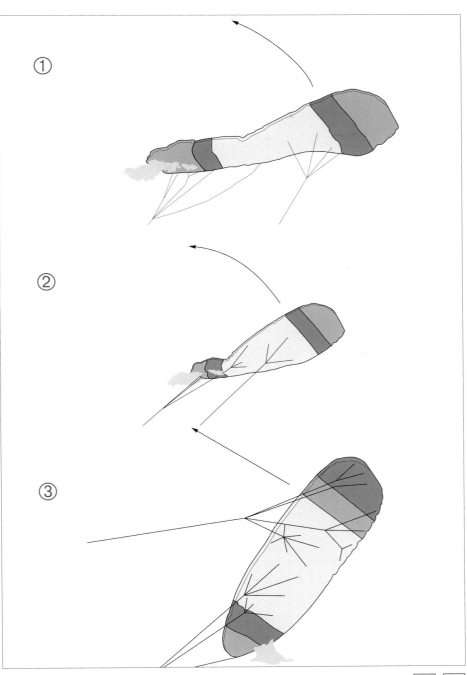

window to the zenith by pulling gently on the upper tip of the kite with the control bar. Then, bring the bar to a 'neutral' position to 'park' the kite there.

Steering

As before, keep the kite high in the window while you get used to how it handles. Turning is done by pulling one side of the bar towards you and pushing the other away, pivoting it around the centre. Pull right to go right, pull left to go left. It will feel different from how the kite flies on four lines, so take some time to accustom yourself to its handling before you hit full power. It's still the same kite, though, and will perform in the same way in terms of how and where in the wind window it pulls. Practice some figure of eight manoeuvres, flying alternate left and right loops, so you can make sure you can do it well to both sides.

Now that it's a two-line kite, you will not be able to slow it down, stop or reverse, of course. If at any stage you need to lose some power, you will need to fly the kite out to the edge of the wind window, either at one side or at the zenith.

Landing

Without the ability to reverse land, this, too, will need to be done differently from landing a four-line kite. You can self-land in light to moderate winds and, in fact, the technique is the same as that for landing a basic Flexifoil kite.

- with the kite flying up the centre of the wind window, pull on one side of the control bar to execute a loop.
- when the kite has made half of its loop and is pointing towards the other side of the wind window, bring the control bar to neutral and fly a low horizontal pass, taking the kite out to that side of the wind window.
- keep flying it in that direction until it loses power, steering it towards the ground. It will fall to the ground when it is out of the window.
- quickly go and retrieve your kite, weighting it down with sand or whatever comes to hand, but not sharp or pointed objects. Otherwise, it can easily blow away.
- safety note: **Do not attempt to self-land in a strong wind as you will almost certainly never be able to retrieve the kite before it blows away. You will need a helper to grab the kite and immobilize it for you. Follow the steps below.**

Fly the kite out to one side of the wind window as described above.
- steer the kite down near to the ground.
- your helper should approach the kite from downwind, behind it, well clear of the lines. Keep the kite as still as possible close to the ground until they are able to grab one tip and then pull the kite down.
- as soon as your helper has immobilized the kite by weighting it down with sand or similar, you should release the tension on the flying lines by taking a couple of steps forwards towards the kite. You can stake it down using the loop at the rear if you wish.

◀ *Kiteboard gymnastics on a four-line control bar*

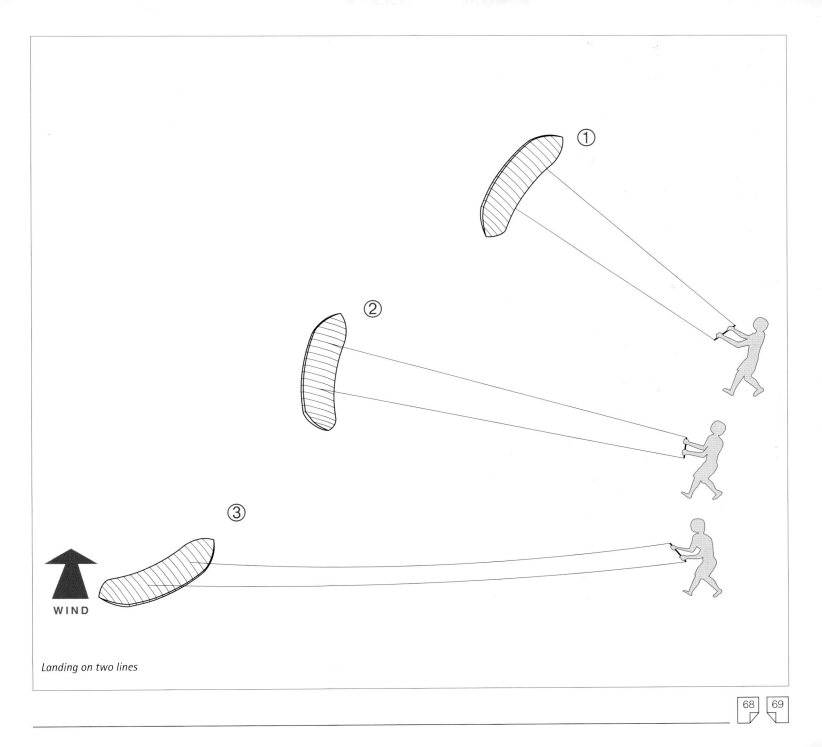

Landing on two lines

Buggying

"Moving with the wind the first time you bomb down the beach is just awesome. Then you suddenly think 'how do I stop?!' but it helps amazingly for making the transition on to a kiteboard."

Andreya Wharry
Professional kiteboarder and power kite instructor

What is kite buggying?

THE IDEA IS VERY simple. Fly a large single kite, or stack of smaller ones, that generate enough power to pull yourself along. Sit in your vehicle and, attaching the kites to you or the vehicle, manipulate them in such a way as to pull you and it along.

A modern power kite and kite buggy are sophisticated adrenaline sport tools specifically designed for the job, generating speeds of up to 50 mph. They are the result of more than 15 years of intensive commercial research and development. When you sit down in a kite buggy with the control handles in your hands, you know you're in for a thrill. It's an immense buzz travelling along low down, open to the elements. Even your first 5 mph run feels like 50. A bang up-to-date toy in all respects, but moving around by kite power is by no means a new idea.

It's a much repeated story, but one worth telling again. The idea of using kite power on a wheeled vehicle is anything but new. During the late eighteenth century, in the south west of England around Bristol, George Pocock was experimenting with kite traction using large kites attached to a carriage.

About 200 years later, despite Andrew Jones and Ray Merry's best early efforts at getting mobile, their long-standing traction addict friend, New Zealander Peter Lynn, is widely credited with being the inventor of a successful modern kite vehicle. He came up

◄ *Flexifoil's production buggy*

▶ *An original Peter Lynn buggy*

with a single-seater, three-wheeled buggy, with the driver sitting low to the ground over the rear axle, flying kites with his hands and steering the single front wheel with his feet. The kite used was a modern, two-lined, soft aerofoil kite called a Peel, on account of its pointed, eliptical shape, which resembles a slice of orange peel.

The buggy frame was stainless steel and used high-quality bearings. Its simple basket-style seat meant that it was very easy to be pulled out of the buggy, leading to many spectacular wipeouts. The kites were not specifically designed for the job — they just happened to be what was available at the time.

Kite power existed and people were hunting around for something to do with it. The whole package was far from perfect, but, nevertheless, kite buggying was born and

has not, in essence, changed format since, despite the countless buggies and traction kites that are on the market today.

The first Lynn buggies appeared in the mid to late 1980s, but manufacturing costs were so high that they were very expensive — as were many of the kites used to power them — putting them out of the reach of the average kite flyer. Although the idea of buggying was sold as something you could do anywhere you could find a large, flat area, the reality was that clearly a buggy was most at home on big, hard, sandy beaches or mud and salt flats, where the wind is smooth and you can roll for literally miles.

The buggy scene grew painfully slowly for a while, but grow it steadily did. Then, in 1992, the first soft four-line ram air kites appeared and other kite and buggy manufacturers were starting to get involved as the

Original and sports buggys

sales volumes slowly increased. Flexifoil commissioned its own buggy designs from Peter Lynn in 1994, then launched its Skytiger series in 1995 and suddenly buggying took off big time.

Within a couple of years, a full national and international competition race circuit, club and society network had grown up as, all of a sudden, kite buggying began to appeal to adrenaline sportspeople from beyond the kite scene. The surge of interest in the mid 1990s brought in new and different ideas and equipment developed fast. Needless to say, Flexifoil has been at the forefront of the whole traction scene, supporting events and organizations, sponsoring drivers (and now kiteboarders) and so on. Products have developed at an astonishing rate and kite buggying is a vastly different beast nowadays. There are three ranges of kites that can be used for buggying

available from Flexifoil alone and it's a highly specialized business.

The latest Flexifoil buggy by Rob Hills is an even more robust design than previous incarnations following extensive R&D work and is designed for even more extreme usage, especially jumping with the buggy. It features an adjustable downtube on the front fork to cater for most sizes of rider, curved footrests to help keep your feet in position, a high-grade, wide, stainless steel tube frame for strength, a wraparound seat for comfort and back support, stainless steel bolts and specially engineered fittings. It's an absolutely bang up-to-date model and typical of its kind, see page 72.

Buggying's natural habitat is the beach so a logical next step was to go on the water, too, and this has now happened with kiteboarding. You could argue that the water version would never have happened without buggying sorting so many issues out before-

hand. The surf version has somewhat eclipsed buggying of late – mediawise at least – but that can't hide the fact that more and more people are coming to buggying, too, as part of the big wave of interest in kite traction tomfoolery.

The rules of the road

Let's say this now because, before you go anywhere near a buggy, you need to understand a few things. Good buggying means safe and responsible buggying because the danger to yourself and other people is considerable. Here are some golden rules.

- do not attempt to kite buggy until you have fully mastered your kite.
- never attach yourself permanently to the kite.
- use extreme caution.
- never use your buggy in conditions that are

too extreme for your skill level and equipment.

- never kite buggy if you cannot safely handle the power of your kite — use a smaller kite or wait for lighter wind.
- avoid gusty winds, which can be very difficult for inexperienced flyers.
- avoid all other kite contraindications — lightning, power cables, roads, airports and so on.
- always disable your kite and lines when not in use and avoid leaving unsecured kites on the ground.
- never buggy on busy beaches or anywhere you could injure someone — the more deserted it is the better.
- always obtain permission to use the site if appropriate.
- respect nature, the site and other users at all times, always clearing up your rubbish.
- check all your equipment regularly — kites, buggy, flying lines, harness and other safety gear — and especially carefully before use.
- do not use worn or damaged equipment — repair or replace it immediately.
- always use appropriate safety equipment.
- be aware of your flying lines at all times. These can cause serious injury when under tension from a powered-up kite.
- never allow inexperienced kite flyers to use your equipment. Take out third-party liability insurance that covers buggying.

In short, use your common sense. There will be plenty of buzz to come without taking unnecessary risks.

▶ *Flexifoil buggy in action*

▲ *Trick style: Two wheel riding*

▶ *A big foot buggy*

Getting started

You'll want the right kind of kite for buggying and what that almost certainly means is:

- four lines, so you can 'lock' the kite in the power zone and regulate the power by changing the angle of attack
- a relatively thin profile to reduce lateral pull
- a big wind window to make getting back upwind easier
- mobility around the window to guarantee continuous access to maximum power
- good edge handling and performance
- smooth (as opposed to abrupt) acceleration to reduce the tendency to pull the driver out of the buggy.

Flexifoils make models that fit the bill, and you've already made one good buggying decision before you start.

It's possible to learn buggying on your own — after all, the people who invented it had to make it up as they went along — but a good idea might be to try one of the Flexifoil-approved buggy schools. There you can learn the basics and try out different equipment in complete (and insured!) safety before committing your cash.

When you're ready to have a go in your own time, you will need to have your own buggy, which may be a Flexifoil model or one of the many others on the market. Follow the manufacturer's instructions for assembling whatever buggy you get. Make sure the wheels are tightly bolted on and the tyres inflated to the correct pressure.

There are three different widths of tyres you can fit to your buggy. The most common are the standard width ones (see page 72) but the wider version which fit the Flexifoil buggy spread the load over a wide area and prevent the buggy sinking in the sand. Even so, for very soft sand you might one day want to invest in a set of giant 'big foot' wheels, which can be fitted on to a standard Flexifoil buggy rear axle. The third option — rarely used generally and not at all by Flexifoil — is narrow wheels. These are good for hard ground or even road-type surfaces, such as old airfields.

Like all aspects of power kiting, you are better advised to start learning in a light to moderate wind, up to 15 mph. Then, the kite will pull less and everything will be happening slower. You'll need to multitask and there's definitely a bit of brain overload to begin with as you get used to controlling the kite and buggy simultaneously, so slowing everything down a bit can really help.

Check the wind direction carefully, especially if you're using a coastal site. The best wind on a beach will be an onshore one, coming on to the beach from the sea. Not only will it be smooth, as the aim will be to 'sail' backwards and forwards across the wind, it will allow you to run up and down the length of the beach and keep out of the water. An offshore wind will probably be lumpy and drive you out into the water more.

Clearly, you're going to need a vastly bigger space than ever before, especially while you're learning and can't fully control what you do.

Here's what you need to do and refer to the diagrams on page 78.

- 1. Your buggy should be pointing at 45 degrees to the wind direction, downwind, to help you get going.
- once the buggy is moving, you will be trying to steer across the wind so as not to lose too much ground forwards. You can run downwind but you're going to have a long and uncomfortable walk back, carrying all that equipment with the wind against you. Your first objective is to learn how to buggy across the wind.
- launch your kite and take it to the minimum power position at the zenith while you approach the buggy from the downwind side. This is to avoid you suddenly being pulled forwards by a big gust, causing you to fall on the buggy.
- keeping the kite at the zenith, straddle the buggy and sit down in it. At this point you still have some resistance from your feet.
- put one foot (upwind) on its foot peg, the other still holding you from being pulled forwards.
- 2. You are committed to going towards the side the buggy is pointing, so carefully steer the kite down the edge of the window you want to go towards. Never take the kite back to the other side of the window as this will result in you being pulled backwards out of the buggy.
- as you feel the power coming into the kite, lift your other foot up on to its foot peg. If the buggy does not begin to move, steer it down wind, but not too much or the flying lines will become slack.
- 3. 'Lock' the kite in position at roughly 45

degrees to the ground and keep tension on the flying lines as the buggy gets going to avoid running over your own lines. Try to steer the buggy more across the wind. Remember to watch where you're going as well as the kite. You should be flying on the front lines mostly, just using the rear lines to hold the kite in position. If you're going too fast, take the kite further up the wind window, which will reduce its power and slow you down.

- keeping moving is easier in a reasonable, steady wind than in a light wind. As the kite comes down the edge of the wind window, it wants to power you in that direction. You lock your kite at 45 degrees to the ground and try to steer the buggy slightly up and across the wind. In a light wind, you will need to 'work' the kite more, flying a continuous figure of eight pattern on the edge of the window. This is easier said than done when you're also watching for other site users and so on.

The tuning of your four-line kite becomes apparent very quickly as it will give — if it's correctly set up — the ability to hit the brakes very hard for an instant depowering, even to land the kite, if it all gets too much. More significantly, however, it's the four-line control that allows you to lock the kite in position. That's why four-line kites are so popular, helping you reduce the brain overload so you can concentrate more on buggying.

Another factor that comes into play once you start moving forwards across the wind is the phenomenon of 'apparent wind'. Imagine you are sitting in the buggy, pointing at

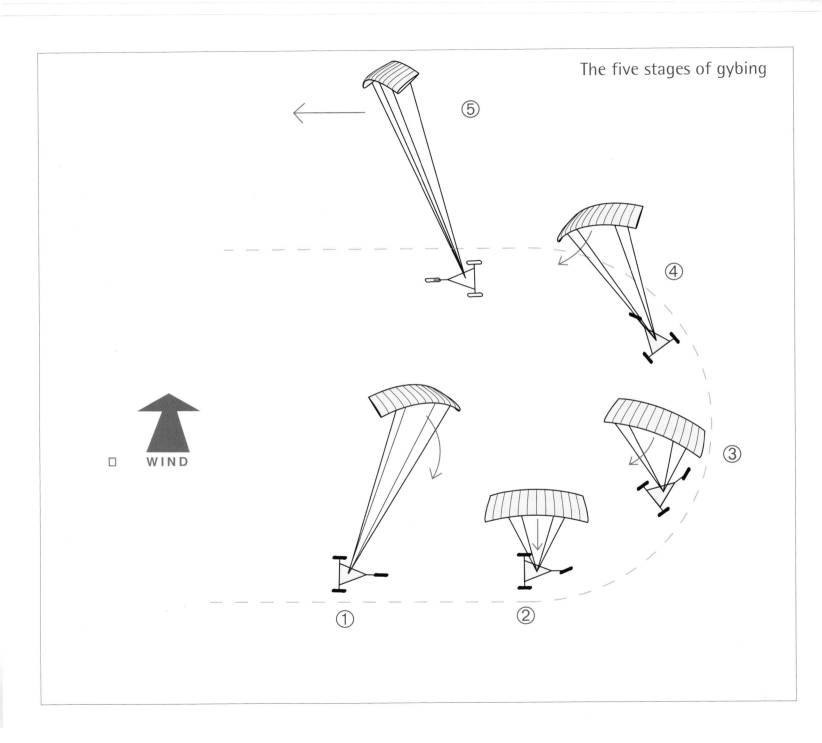

The five stages of gybing

WIND

① ② ③ ④ ⑤

Gybing

This odd word, borrowed from sailing, means turning the buggy through 180 degrees to go back the way you came. No matter how good a time you're having, you will have to do this at some time or another. Thinking about it, how you do this is not at all obvious. The kite's in front of you, nicely powered up, but what do you do with it next to get it back to the other side of the wind window without being pulled out of the buggy? Which way do you turn the buggy anyway – up- or downwind? My car's four miles back up the beach. Help!

You can turn up- or downwind, but upwind is an advanced technique so we'll concentrate on the downwind version. Like all manoeuvres, it's one that needs good timing and adjustment all the way through. The first and most important thing you'll need to adjust is your forward speed. You can't really learn how to turn going in at full speed and you'll need to lose some before you turn anyway. The main thing to remember is always to turn downwind, towards the kite. You need to turn the buggy as quickly as possible. Actually turning the buggy is very easy as your feet are steering directly through the front wheel. There's no counter-steering against the pull. See opposite page.

- 1 and 2. You are driving your buggy on a cross-wind reach with the kite powered up and 'locked' at 45 degrees to the ground. Start steering the kite up the edge of the wind window. The power eases off a little and the buggy starts to lose speed.

- 3. You're ready to make your turn. Steer the kite back up the wind window to the centre, leading edge pointing straight upwards. At the same time, steer the buggy hard into the turn. You need to use full lock to bring the buggy round quickly.

- 4. As the buggy comes round 180 degrees and is pointing back the way you came, start steering the kite over to the other side of the wind window, the side you want to move towards.

- 5. Let the buggy get going again downwind slightly, then neutralize your buggy steering and steer the kite to the correct position to 'lock' it on the edge for your return reach. Be ready for the pull coming back on as the kite powers back up again.

There's a fine balance to strike to make a good turn. You must slow down beforehand, but you've also got to make sure you go in with enough speed to get all the way through the turn or you risk being pulled out of the buggy. If the buggy stops moving, then the moment when the kite powers up again is when you could be yanked face forwards out of and across your buggy.

As you make your downwind turn, you come face on to the kite. If you travel too far downwind or too fast, you will depower the kite, causing it to deflate and start to fall from the sky. Two things are then likely to happen. First, as the kite sinks, your flying lines fall on the ground, you run over them with the buggy and, hey presto, 293 twists of line round your axle. Second, with no kite to pull it, the buggy slows down, bringing tension back on to the flying lines, the kite reinflates and the power kicks back in, but now it's low down in the window, right in the power zone, and pulls you face forwards out of your buggy as it does so. If either of these happens, then you're in big trouble as the kite will be almost impossible to control with its lines snagged round the axle. You will have to forget about the handles and try to retrieve and control the kite before you can sort out the mess. That's why it's important to try and get the buggy round its turn as quickly as you can.

Most people's problems with turning arise from lack of forward speed going in or from going too far downwind in the turn. With practice, you'll be able to make your turns faster, keeping more power in the kite. Clearly, too, you're going to need to practice turning to both sides — for your own convenience and in case you need to take emergency avoidance action. Soon you'll be ready for some power turns, which come a lot easier if you've fully mastered the power stop and slide. The difference here is that you're going to be sliding downwind, towards the kite.

- you are driving the buggy fast on a cross-wind reach. Steer the kite quickly up the edge of the window and to a position high in it with the leading edge pointing straight up.
- as you do so, slam the buggy into a full 180-degree turn, steering the kite over to the other side of the window to its 'locked' position where it will quickly power up again.
- reverse your buggy steering to counter the pull, putting it into a skid. Then, quickly neutralize the buggy steering to accelerate

away from the turn on an opposite reach, bringing the kite to its 45-degree angle to the ground.

The trick is to be quick with the kite so that the moment when you are face on to the kite and it is quite powered up passes quickly. The kite will still, briefly, be behind you, this time with more power. You will be powering into the corner and it will be more difficult to turn the buggy, so you need good leg strength and quick feet to whip the buggy round fast. With more power, you will need to lean against the kite, making a lot of work for your lower back and upper body. The advantage of a power turn is that, if you get it right, obviously it's much faster and you lose less ground downwind than with the other methods described earlier.

Getting up wind

Once you've established enough control over what you're doing in the buggy to be able to reach backwards and forwards across the wind, you will want to learn how to make that into steady upwind tacking. However well you learn to get upwind, it is always going to be slow progress and you must be patient and prepared to work the kite and buggy to get where you want to go.

Getting back upwind is the hardest thing to learn as a buggy driver, so, if you find it difficult at first, stick with it because patience will definitely bring its rewards. Initially, as you learn to drive, you will find that your reaches take you gradually downwind. To get back upwind, you will need to steer more aggressively with your feet, try-

ing to keep the buggy pointing slightly upwind on each tack, at the same time being less aggressive with the kite. You need to keep the kite less powered up by keeping it higher than normal on the edge of the wind window. Depending on the terrain you may need to move the kite up and down to generate enough pull to gain ground. There's that apparent wind factor to consider also. Again, there's a fine balance to achieve because if you're travelling too slowly and haven't got enough power you'll also find it difficult. This is particularly so during the turn at the end of each tack. The turns are made downwind as normal and if you lose speed or stop, you're going to have to give up some of your hard-won ground upwind, going slightly downwind to get the buggy moving again. You need to make the turns as tight as possible — if you can, steering a little more upwind just before the turn and turning through more than 180 degrees to get on another upwind tack.

If it sounds difficult, that's because it is. Once you've mastered this, though, you've got a full hand of buggy manoeuvres and a whole adventure playground of kite-powered possibilities will open up for you.

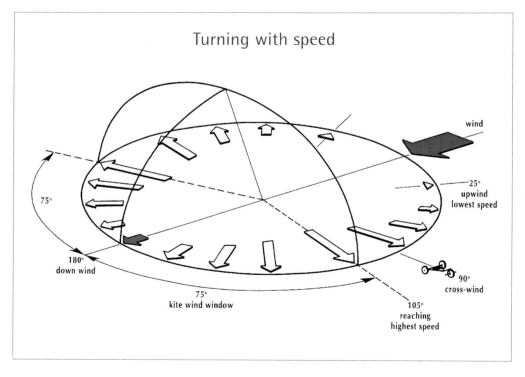

Turning with speed

wind

25°
upwind
lowest speed

75°

180°
down wind

75°
kite wind window

90°
cross-wind

105°
reaching
highest speed

Essential and optional buggying equipment

There's an awful lot more to good buggying than simply having a kite and a buggy. There are all sorts of other bits and pieces you might want to have that will make your buggying easier and more enjoyable. It's not simply a question of fun, first and foremost – there's the safety aspect, protecting yourself and others from the worst case scenario because you're playing with big power and anything can happen. When you see a buggy driver fully kitted out nowadays, ready to race in all weathers, they may have as many as 50 different extra bits on top of the essential kite and buggy.

Essentials
- a crash helmet, which protects you from hitting other objects or being hit by the buggy.
- strong shoes – your feet take a lot of wear and tear.
- knee, elbow and wrist guards, which protect vulnerable joints from knocks and hard landings.
- suitable eyewear – sunglasses to protect from ultraviolet light and glare, but, more likely, goggles to keep sand and spray out of your eyes.
- gloves.
- ground stake for immobilizing your kite.

▸ *Top: Crash helmet/sun glasses*
▸ *Middle: Knee pads*
▸ *Bottom: Elbow pads*

Optional
- waterproof clothing – some kind of a spray suit.
- thermal clothing to wear underneath the waterproof clothes.
- face guard to protect from spray
- scarf to protect from spray. This and the face guard can help prevent some nasty skin infections you pick up from some 'dirty' coastal sites.
- ankle straps with a ground stake sheath.
- wind meter.
- harness and harness loop, which are invaluable if you want to buggy for long periods and/or in really big winds. You should not consider trying a harness until you have fully mastered the basic elements of kite buggying, though.
- large ground stake (stake for tethering dogs to or other) for keeping several different-sized kites immobilized, but ready to fly at one time on days of changeable winds.
- line equalizer to quickly test if your flying lines have stretched and by how much.
- a quick-release system for depowering the kite in an emergency without letting go completely.
- chest protector.
- shin guards.
- beach tent or cabana to store spare equipment in and get out of the wind for a rest at times when you can't take your vehicle on to the beach.
- a back rest, because it can be very hard work for your lower back.
- foot peg straps, which will help stop your feet 'bouncing' off the pegs as you go over bumps or round turns.

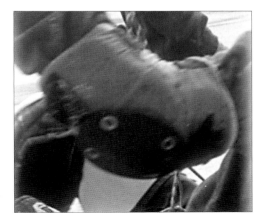

- a speedometer so you know how fast you're going.
- a compass to know which direction you're travelling in.
- splash guards to reduce the spray problem.
- rear kit bag to carry spare kite and lines.
- giant soft sand tyres.
- buggy belt to strap yourself in for some jumps on the sand dunes or simply to hold you in at moments of extreme power — these times can be extremely dangerous.
- tandem kit for attaching another buggy to the rear of your buggy — there is theoretically no limit to how many buggies could be attached in a 'tandem'.
- extended rear axle to help reduce sideways skids.
- teflon-based lubricant (bike chain spray) for maintenance of the bearings.

This list seems long already, but we haven't even started looking at all the things like spare control handles or bars and flying lines, spare buggy parts, toolkit, sailcloth repair tape and kits, flying line sleeving and splicing kit ...

It goes without saying that kite buggying is not really a sport you can go and do using public transport — you'll be needing a car or small van at the very least.

▸ *Top: Goggles*

▸ *Middle: Spray guard*

▸ *Bottom: Wind meter*

◀ *Carving up the high water in a buggy*

Other
Land based
activities

5

ONCE THE BASIC PRINCIPLE of kite traction for wheeled transport became established, curiosity naturally drove people to experiment with various other options. Some things were obviously off limits, such as biking — the ability to steer with your hands being somewhat crucial and, in any event, the centre of balance is too high off the ground to be stable. Skateboarding is an obvious contender, but is just too fast and also unstable — there's not enough board to really lean against and, again, the centre of gravity is high. One or two variations are credible and have been successfully commercialized. Flexifoil kites are very well suited to them nevertheless.

Mountainboard

Like a big, off-road skateboard with either a three or four-wheel configuration, these are great fun on any hard beach or big inland open space with reasonably smooth terrain, such as playing fields. A beach — with its advantages of space and smooth wind — is what you really want to help you learn, taking into account the relatively small board surface to grip and high centre of gravity. As usual you'll need a very big space away from other people and obstacles, with plenty of room downwind in case you are pulled forwards.

The same safety equipment as for buggying is recommended, but with even more

◀ *The latest craze: mountainboarding*

▶ *Ripping it up on a Blade-powered mountainboard*

emphasis on the elbow, wrist and knee guards. You won't want a harness to begin with as, if you are pulled over forwards, the hook and its fitting could cause you injury, pushing back against your stomach. Later on you might decide to use a harness and it will certainly help move the centre of pull lower down, hence reducing wasted effort, which means faster, more efficient boarding.

As before, you'll be better off learning in a light to moderate wind where things will happen more slowly than in a big wind. You can afford to be much less powered up than for a buggy, especially on hard, flat sand, as the resistance from a mountainboard is very low. Use a smaller kite to begin with anyway as there will be less lateral pull and you should find it easier to stay up on the board. Tacking and getting upwind are the objectives.

The boards are basically flat, curving up at the front and rear tips, with a grip mat on the deck for the feet. There are several board models. Three-wheeled boards have their single wheel at the rear and cannot reverse, while four-wheeled boards are able to go in both directions. Some have cushioned, neoprene foot strap bindings, which obviously help with leverage, just as they do in windsurfing. It's actually better, though, to learn without the bindings, mastering the basics before you start fixing yourself to the board.

Your final check before stepping on to your board is to see if you are regular or goofy. This means which way you prefer to stand and, in particular, which foot you place forwards when you stand to ride a board. If you don't know, have a friend shove you in the back. Whichever foot you use to save

yourself is your lead foot and the other the supporting foot. Goofy is right foot forward, regular left foot forward. Start off by going towards your good side to make it easier.

Now set up your board as you would for a buggy start, pointing downwind across the window, at 45 degrees to the wind direction, towards your good side.

- launch your kite and fly it up to the minimum power position at the zenith.
- you will need to approach the board from one side or the other. From upwind means you can see where you're putting your feet better than when you're approaching it from downwind — important if you've got bindings to get into — but could trip over the board if pulled by a gust. From downwind means no tripping over, but then you can't see where you put your feet so well. Try from upwind first and see which you prefer.
- you will need to bring the kite down the edge of the window you want to move towards, taking care not to bring the kite too low and risk being pulled off as a result. The board should then move towards the kite and keep moving towards it as long as you keep the kite there. There's a lot of body work to be done, balancing and levering against the kite, and you'll need a good flexed position, knees and arms slightly bent.
- start by steering slightly downwind to get some momentum before gradually easing yourself on to a cross-wind reach. Do this by transferring weight slightly on to your heels.

▶ *Getting some air on a mountainboard*

- You can slow down any time by taking the kite higher in the wind window.

Turning round

There are several ways in which you can do this — all of which will present you with some degree of awkwardness.

If you're using a three-wheeled board, you've got two choices. The first and simplest would be to take your kite up to the zenith to depower it and slow to a stop. Get off your board and turn it round, remount it and ride back the other way as you did before, this time to your 'bad' side, leading with your other foot. The other way involves actually turning the board as you ride along, as follows.

- transfer your weight to your toes and the board will begin to turn downwind, towards the kite. Go carefully — not too much weight too quickly. You are aiming to do a wide, carving, downwind turn.
- as you begin to turn the board, fly the kite up the edge of the window, turning it to point the other way and gradually bringing it across the high part of the window to begin pulling you in the opposite direction, keeping tension on the flying lines.
- keep the weight on your toes as the board comes round 180 degrees.
- bring the kite to the appropriate position and 'lock' it on the edge of the wind window. The kite will power up again and you will accelerate forwards, back the way you came.

It's all a question of timing. The more you practice, the better your timing will be and you'll be able to do the whole thing in one sweeping movement. The advantage here is that you keep moving; the disadvantage is that you're now flying over your lead shoulder with your back to the kite and this will require some practice to get right. The balance changes completely and you're leaning on your toes more.

A four-wheeled board handles differently, more like a twin tip kiteboard for water. It's symmetrical, so you can take advantage of its reversability.

- as you ride along, bring the kite up the wind window where it will act as a brake, slowing you down. Shift your weight slightly to the centre of the board.
- fly the kite across the top of the wind window, turning it to point the other way. As the board stops, bring your weight over on to your 'good' foot so you are now leading with your 'bad' one.
- as you bring the kite down the other edge of the window, it will power up again and you can 'lock' it at the appropriate place for your return reach.

Whichever way you're doing it, with practice you'll be able to make your turns faster and more aggressive, losing less power and speed. Tricks such as jumps and power slides can also be done, especially once you start using bindings.

Stopping

The simplest way to stop your mountainboard is, as explained, to steer the kite up to the zenith and keep it there while you slow to a stop. There's a way of stopping more quickly that is similar to the way you stop a buggy.

- you are reaching across the wind at reasonable speed. Start steering the kite up the edge of the window towards the top of the centre of the wind window.
- as you do so, start applying pressure on the board with your heels to turn the board upwind, keeping the kite high in the middle of the wind window, pointing straight upwards where it will brake your forward speed.
- lean slightly against the pull of the kite to stop your board. Keep the kite up at the zenith with minimum power.

With practice, you'll be able to make the stop much more aggressive, moving the kite slightly earlier and more quickly. Be careful not to get the kite too far behind you or too quickly or too low down — all of which could lead to you being pulled backwards off the board.

Rollerblades

Rollerblading means low resistance, high speed and hard crashes. Not for the faint-hearted, full safety equipment is recommended and the use of small kites only.

This is mostly done on a kind of mountainboard version of roller skates or blades, using mountainboard wheels. One or two companies now manufacture these and you should try skate and kite retailers first, but, if you find them difficult to track down, you're looking at a DIY project.

Blades and skates are a bit more like water skis and wakeboards in so much as you strap yourself in first and then launch the kite to power yourself up. That in itself presents dangers because, if you get into difficulty, you cannot detach yourself from them — you will have to deal with the kite somehow. This said, clearly with such low resistance the potential is there to go very fast and there's surely more freedom of movement for jumps and tricks than is the case with mountain-boards. Time will tell.

Getting started

Being strapped in, you don't want to launch the kite in the centre of the window with full power, so you need to set things up carefully. Work out whether you're regular or goofy, adopt your stance and go in that direction to begin with. Use a small kite in moderate wind and, as before, objective one is to learn to ride backwards and forwards across the wind.

- set the kite up close to the edge of the wind window, on the side that is the direction you want to go in.
- put your blades or skates on, along with your other safety equipment, and get ready to launch the kite, pointing it slightly downwind to help get some momentum. Your feet should be parallel, with your good foot slightly advanced.

▶ *Fast and dangerous — powered Rollerblading*

- launch and fly the kite straight up the edge to the zenith, balancing your body to lever against any pull. If you move forwards a little, do not worry — taking the kite to the zenith will stop you again.
- now, bring the kite slowly down the edge of the wind window on the side you want to move towards. It will begin to power up and you will begin to move forwards. You will need to make lots of body adjustments to lever against the pull. Keep your knees slightly bent, leaning back to lever against the kite.

Stopping

- take the kite up the edge of the wind window towards the zenith, pointing straight up. The kite will be flying slightly behind you and will act as a brake.
- turn your blades to point further upwind, so you're flying over your shoulder. You will quickly come to a stop.
- keep the kite at the zenith or land it right on the edge of the wind window.

An alternative would be to apply full reverse with your rear lines. This should depower the kite immediately and then you can turn your blades upwind while you reverse land the kite.

Turning is done in the same way as has been described for a mountainboard — a wide, sweeping, carve turn done downwind. The only exception is that you can make a transition with your feet so that you're leading with your 'bad' foot. This means you can stay face on to the kite.

Getting big airs with tricks and gymnastics

If you are into getting your airs in a big way, you'll be looking for two things — distance and hang time. The biggest officially recorded jumps have been well over 30 metres (100

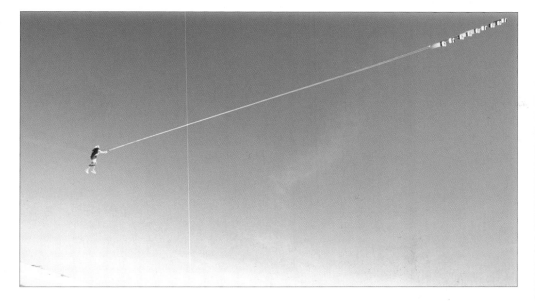

feet) and have been done with the help of full support and back-up teams, not to mention medical assistance on hand if necessary. Stories of even bigger training and accidental jumps abound, with varying degrees of amazing escapes, broken bones and sometimes more serious consequences.

You can use big stacks of Flexis or big, single, traction foils — both will do the job.

The basic idea of the tricks is to start actually using your hang time, in the same way that kiteboarders are doing, to hit some rotations or whatever. Like everything else, try it first in moderate winds with some smaller airs to begin with. You will be landing on hard ground at speed. Build up the power and size of your jumps gradually as you gain skill and confidence.

Single and multiple rotations and somersaults are the general order. Be aware that any sizeable jump is going to result in a very heavy landing, so you really do need to be fully protected with helmet, gloves, strong footwear and elbow, knee and wrist guards. Also, it's very tiring and you won't be able to keep going too long. This is especially so as all your jumps will be taking you downwind, leaving you a stamina-sapping walk back upwind to your start point, trying to keep your kite(s) at the zenith with no power.

Acknowledging the somewhat unhinged nature of this activity, try, even so, to take care with getting your airs. Just like all your other power kiting disciplines, minimize the risk to yourself and others. That way you'll enjoy your power kiting to the max.

◀ *Kitesnow: A good winter option*

▲ *Tethered man lifting on a stack of Flexis. Don't try this at home*

▶ *Time for some tricks*

Kites for
Sea and surf

"I switched to kiteboarding (from windsurfing) for the big airtime. Combined with the bonus of less hassle, kiteboarding has the best bits of wind-surfing times ten."

Chris Calthrop
Flexifoil sponsored kiteboarder

6

OVER THE LAST COUPLE of years, there's been much learned discussion and disagreement about when and where exactly kiteboarding was invented. What's not disputed is that people have been experimenting with kite power on water for years. The current explosion of interest in this new, most radical of extreme sports is simply the result of a long and winding journey that has brought us to where we are now.

The potential was obviously there, it was just the formula that had to be perfected. Flexifoil experimented with the kiteboat — Jacob's Ladder, described earlier, and other previous aquatic efforts. Elsewhere in the world, other people had tried water skis and adapted buggies, fitting floats in place of the wheels. Of all these, Corey Roesler's 'Kiteski' rig — dual water skis with a large, framed kite and a motorized winding, recovery and relaunch system on a control bar, which was up and running in 1993 — was the most workable. However, it was not commercially successful. It was ahead of its time in many ways.

The general consensus nowadays seems to be that kiteboarding was actually done successfully first in the south of France, on the coast near Montpellier, some time around 1996 or 1997. From there it was exported, mainly by one man — Manu Bertin — to Hawaii, or, more correctly, Maui, to where the likes of legendary futuristic surfer Laird Hamilton and his group were also trying to

◄ *Kiteboarding: The Ultimate wind-water buzz*

► *One of the original water men – Corey Roesler*

make kiteboarding happen. This small group of power kiters and surf freaks used adapted surfboards and the kind of big wings that were about at the time. They mostly consisted of big ram air wings, such as the two-line Peels, four-line Skytigers and then the Blade, which followed soon after. Kiteboarding has now been successfully exported from France and Hawaii to dozens of countries around the world.

Clearly there was one big issue that had not really cropped up in kiting before to any great extent, other than in an experimental or demonstration sense. This issue was water relaunching. A big ram air wing is made with big vents along the front that take in water just as effectively as they do air. The ripstop fabric is covered with a waterproof coating,

but, after more than a few minutes lying flat on the water, the whole sail becomes waterlogged and impossible to relaunch without gathering it all up, swimming back in, drying it out and starting again.

There was another issue — getting back upwind. Early kiteboarders spent a lot of time carrying their gear back from downwind. This was a result of the combination of not yet having the skill and not being able to find the kind of wing or board that could make that possible.

The basic point here is that, once again, what people were doing out there was running ahead of product development. They were using what kites were available rather than some specifically designed for the job. The Blade was an interim response to their

needs, with fewer vents along the leading edge and an eliptical shape.

In a light wind, there's still very little to beat a big ram air wing. In other wind conditions, however, there's another system that has swept all before it, in the competitive sense, filling the podium positions at nearly all the major kiteboarding events in the last couple of years.

In 1984, French brothers Bruno and Dominique Legaignoux patented a system for putting sealed inflatable tube stiffeners in a single-skinned sail that could be flown as a kite on two lines attached directly to the wing's tips, the inflatable sections rendering it effectively unsinkable. Like all great ideas, it is very simple. The wing, though some way from the finished product, flew OK, pulled hard enough to cope with the resistance of rider on water and was, technically speaking, fully water relaunchable. The inflatable tube stiffeners — one along the leading edge and a series of vertical battens — have dual functions, serving as frame and buoyancy.

The Legaignoux brothers always believed in the possibility of kiteboarding, trying many experiments themselves over the years. When kiteboarders saw the potential, they started using the kites. Within a couple of years, inflatable kites had been fully adapted for kiteboarding and now command nearly the entire market.

As the inflatable wing idea started to win converts and market share, so, crucially, other big windsurfing manufacturers getting into kiteboarding at that time — particularly

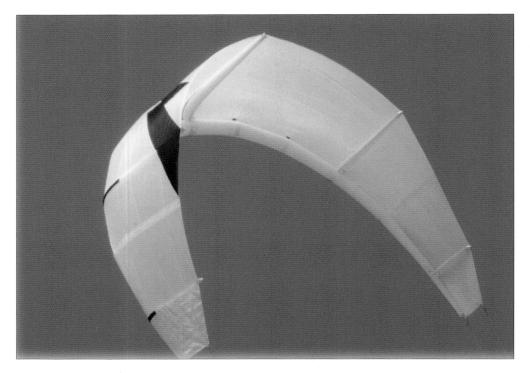

Storm prototype in testing

opinion formers like Naish and Cabrinha — decided that inflatable was the way to go, bought a licence and started making kites. The rest, as they say, is history as a huge list of manufacturers have followed the inflatable route in the face of overwhelming competition success and consumer demand for that type of wing. They make up around 80 per cent of the total market for kiteboard wings. That list now includes Flexifoil International, which has bought a licence and produces its own typically Flexifoil-styled variant of the classic inflatable wing — the Storm.

Inflatable wings are very much a central part of kiteboarding at present. Their tough build and the huge arched shape they take

up in flight are very impressive. As the wing has stiffeners, there's no need for complex bridles and so it's back to the simplicity of flying lines being attached directly to the wing tips.

Although they rule the market at the moment, there's no telling how things will look in a few years' time. Kiteboarding is a very young sport generally and is developing so fast that, as far as the future is concerned, anything is possible.

One thing, sadly, is quite possible, given kiteboarding's current high media profile and commercial success. It is general wing design piracy and/or infringement of the inflatable wing patent. The wing is such an overwhelmingly successful concept that you

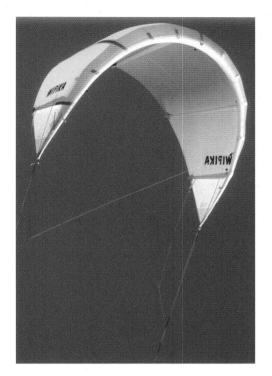

system. If you are ever offered a new Storm or other curved inflatable wing that doesn't bear this certificate, contact Flexifoil International at once or report it to the patent holders at their website (www.inflatablekite.com), including as much information you can about where and when you saw it.

Inflatable kites are increasingly sophisticated, which is not surprising with so many companies working on the same basic system. Most can now be used with either two or four lines. Many have built-in depowering systems, allowing you to adjust the pull while in motion by changing the angle of attack of the kite against the wind. They're all designed to make getting back upwind easier and, needless to say, they exist in a huge range of sizes, tending to be somewhat larger in surface area than ram airs that generate equivalent levels of power in order to compensate for their arched shape.

Competition wings are very elongated — they have a very high aspect ratio. Beginners' inflatable wings tend to have lower aspect ratios and be more rounded in shape. In these respects they conform exactly with the normal principles of kites. What goes around has indeed come around again with this reversion to the simple approach and the latest vogue for two-line flying.

The same is true of flying line control systems. Control bars are very much back in fashion now that they have been successfully adapted to take two-, four- and even three-line set-ups incorporating quick-release safety systems.

In kiteboarding, there are far bigger wings and power in the equation than other kite

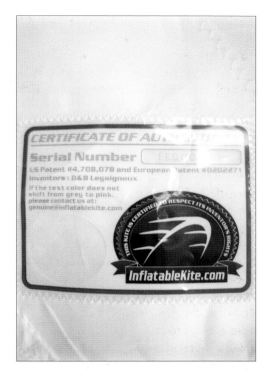

can see why unscrupulous manufacturers might want to shortcut the legal procedure and start manufacturing without a licence or simply rip off an existing design. For this reason, from 2002 onwards, all officially licensed inflatable wing designs will carry a hologramed certificate of authenticity that can't be forged and this both identifies them as legitimate and guarantees their quality of manufacture.

All licensees, including Flexifoil, are cooperating with the new system in an effort to limit the potential for rogue products, which could ultimately endanger lives, entering the

▲ *The original: A Wipika inflatable kite*

▶ *The markings of an original inflatable kite*

sports, so harnesses are a must if we are to fly for any length of time. In the early days, people used windsurfers' harnesses, but now specific kite harnesses are being manufactured to deal with the different kinds of loading and power that kites create. Harness loops of different lengths attached to the handles or control bar are used for different elements of riding. Nevertheless, there are times when it's better to be unhooked in case you get into difficulties and are unable to unhook at that point.

Honourable mention should be made of two other types of kite that have worked well and, in one case, continue to carve their own niche in the busy kiteboarding scene. The first is another Peter Lynn invention —

the C-Quad. This is a kind of hybrid with a flat single skin and a series of carbon fibre battens and stiffeners. The other is an inflatable kite system that is flat rather than arched — the Manta concept, devised by Frenchman Eric Saurre.

Being flat, they develop pull without needing to be made in the bigger sizes that their arched counterparts come in. Some other manufacturers have tried similar wings, including a short-lived Flexifoil project called the Nexus. Both C-Quad and Manta-type kites have been good sellers and played an important part in the development of the sport. Frustratingly for them, however, both struggle for market share against the currently all-conquering arched inflatable wings.

The Storm

"If any kite would get me off Blades, it would be the Storm. It's more durable and has more style. That's the Flexifoil tradition of quality."

Danny Seales
Flexifoil-sponsored kiteboarder

The Storm has been developed largely by Cambridge University aerodynamics graduate and new addition to the Flexifoil design team Henry Rebbeck, with input and assistance from Flexifoil's cofounder Andrew Jones, working from the original Legaignoux concept. It's a typical inflatable wing model, not having any specific aerodynamic fea-

▲ *The Flexfoil Storm production model*

tures that are distinct from other inflatable wings, and Flexifoil hasn't yet tried to make any significant advances of its own to the general concept.

Being a big player in the kite industry is one thing. Competing with some of the heavyweights from the surfing and windsurfing industries is quite another. It's potentially a potent mix of past experiences, kites, boards, windsurfing, coming together to drive the new sport forwards. In this environment, Flexifoil has looked to one of its biggest strengths — that of having taken power kiting to the widest possible market — when developing the Storm.

There are plenty of beginners' wings on the market and plenty more cutting-edge competition wings besides. The Storm fills a huge gap that existed for riders who've passed the elementary stage, aren't looking for a podium place on the pro tours but want the kind of wing that will do for them the kinds of things the pro riders do. A wing that works well, that is simple and efficient to fly, that is fully water relaunchable, built to a high standard, good value and comes with the kind of full before and after sales advice and service that established companies with many years' experience can offer.

Since they were first licensed, there's been

Storm Specifications/Sizes				
Kite size	Flat Area (sqm)	Projected Area (sqm)	Equivalent Wipika Sizing (Flat Area/1.36)	Aspect Ratio
6	6.0	3.7	4.4	5.5
8	8.0	5.1	5.9	6.0
10	10.0	6.1	7.4	6.2
12	12.0	7.3	8.8	6.3
14	14.0	8.6	10.3	6.4
16	16.0	9.6	11.8	6.5

a lot of confusion regarding curved inflatable wing sizes (it's different with ram airs and the Manta type as they are held flatter by their bridle structures), with different manufacturers using different, and quite legitimate, systems for measuring wing size. We're talking about the surface area of a wing type that, though flat when on the ground deflated, has a significant curve when inflated ready for launch and even more so in flight.

The Legaignoux brothers, who hold the inflatable wing patent, have now asked their licensees to end customer confusion by all working to the same system and this should be the case from 2002 onwards. The system uses the 'developed' — also referred to as the 'projected' — area. That's a calculation based on the area of ground covered by the wing's shadow when in flight. The other options are the 'flat' area — the area of ground covered by the wing when it is laid out flat on the ground — and the 'real' area — the total

actual flat surface of fabric used to make the wing. The wingspan sizes given for the Storm are based on the 'real' area. All these different methods of measurement make for highly confusing shopping, to say the least.

The sail itself is made from tough ripstop polyester sailcloth, which is well known for its durability and low stretch. The inflatable tubes are made from polyurethane and the pockets they fit into from polyester laminate.

The wing is built for durability in extreme conditions and so is heavily reinforced at all the wear and tear points — notably the leading edge, trailing edge, line attachments and wing tips. All in all, it's designed and built specifically for kiteboarding at its most efficient as the sport stands today. It will do the job for some time to come, almost certainly, as there's no sign yet of a totally convincing alternative to inflatable wings such as the Storm.

▶ Henry Rebbeck, one of the Storm's designers

Kiteboards

"Over a short time, boards have changed loads. Directionals now come with two straps so you stand more in the centre, better for toe side riding. In flat water and strong wind the wake is the perfect craft. No gybing is a great plus point for twin tips — makes life a lot easier. Now everyone's trying to develop one board with the best points of each."

Jason Furness
Flexifoil-sponsored kiteboarder

In the beginning of kiteboarding, the kites were lacking a little and took time to adapt and the boards didn't exist at all. Most early kiteboard efforts were made on home-adapted surf or windsurf boards. All used some kind of foot bindings — essential for working against the pull of the kites. These were OK in that they got the sport up and running, but weren't designed for the specific strains and loading of kiteboarding. This was especially apparent when it came to jumping or, more specifically, the landings after jumps.

Of course, it didn't take long for shapers and manufacturers from within the established sports of surfing and windsurfing — especially the latter — to start to look seriously at the new sport. Soon, kite-specific boards started to appear, reinforced for kite power.

▲ *Early directional kiteboards*

▶ *The Flexifoil 'loose unit' kiteboard*

With its obvious link to windsurfing, most early kiteboards conformed to the directional principle. That is to say, they were made to go in one direction only. They were classic boards with plenty of volume to keep you afloat and a three-fin configuration at the rear for stability, course holding and control. Being monodirectional (forwards only) meant that they had to be turned round for you to get back to your start point. The objective then was to go backwards and forwards across the wind, even upwind, skill level, board, kite and conditions allowing. Gybing was as much an essential requirement as beach starting, water relaunching and getting up on the board in the first place.

Just as some kiteboarders came to the sport from windsurfing, so others had had prior experience of wakeboard riding. Wakeboards are short and very thin, designed for trick riding. The rider is strapped into full foot

bindings, like those on a snowboard, and towed behind a power boat, playing and tricking on the boat's wake. It didn't take wakeboarders long to realize that you could use the same board with a big kite for power. You could even use a similar control bar to steer the kite. Now the standard 15-minute pay-per-tow can become a session that lasts as long as there's wind available.

Wakeboards are made for a much 'trickier' style of riding than surfboards. Being much shorter and less voluminous means that riders needed to be super powered up to stay afloat. Wakeboards are also normally symmetrical lengthways, having fins at both ends to allow riders to lead with either foot during trick sessions. The implication for kiteboarding was immense. If the board can lead in either direction, this could mean that there'd be no more turning round. To go back the other way you simply reverse your direction. The downside is that, being so small, fast and radical and needing as much wing power as they do, wakeboards are not really suitable for beginners. Also, being strapped in to your foot bindings can make life a bit scary if you do get into difficulties.

It was clear to see from this that what was required was a symmetrical board with sufficient volume for stability and fins at both ends for reversability. The boards duly started to appear during late 2000 — the first developed by top French rider Franz Olry. 'Twin tip' mania was born.

Kiteboarding had finally established its

▶ *Top: Wakeboard action*

▶ *Bottom: A custom twin tip board*

individuality and could be seen to be different from windsurfing because you can't twin tip a windsurfing board. With kite power, you want to turn round. To do this, you slow the board down almost to a stop and quickly, before it can sink, shift your weight and get the wing and it going in the opposite direction. You can still turn round if you want and ride on the other, front side edge for your return, but then you'll be flying over your shoulder with your back to the kite. In surf sports, the front side is what's in front of your toes and the back side is what's behind your heels.

This explains the kiteboarding board family as it is today – directionals, wakeboards and twin tips. The first general principle is big board, small wind; small board, big wind. A big-volume board in a big wind is just too much to handle and a small board in a small wind might well sink due to lack of flotation or power to keep it up.

Mini twin tips and wakeboards are all the rage with experienced riders, and new mini directionals are giving the old format a new lease of life. Mini boards are great for fast action on the water and trickery in the air, giving rise to a radical skateboard style with lots of grabbed 'one-foots' and 'no-foots' – that's jumping and holding the board, taking one or both feet out of the straps and back in again before landing (that kind of thing's not possible on a wakeboard because your feet are strapped in).

The other general board principle is that you should learn on a bigger-volume board as it will be slower, more stable and keep you afloat better than one of the smaller ones. It is also wise to stick to light to moderate winds until you build up your skill and confidence levels. Small boards and big winds are not for beginners.

With the change in style of boards has come a change in style of riding. Where the big-volume directionals are great for planing, small twin tips, and especially wakeboards, are ridden much more aggressively on the edges. Competition riding – which has caught so much media coverage and public interest – really only exists in two formats, at least on the major tours. There is freestyle, which is free riding with the emphasis on tricks and fluid riding, and hang time, which involves riders seeing who can stay up in the air longest (not necessarily the result of the biggest jump).

Board shaping for kites is now big business and most of the big surfing and windsurfing manufacturers have ranges of dedicated kiteboards – that is, they are distinct from their other products. Some have the fins that play such a vital role in controlling the board.

Board evolution is by no means complete. On the contrary, in many ways it's only just beginning. There's talk of new revolutionary shapes that enable you to ride with no side slide, for example. With a sport that's so young and the speed of development so rapid, anything really is possible.

▸ *Setting up your Storm 1-6*

▸ *Far right: Unwinding your lines*

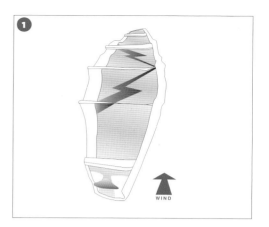

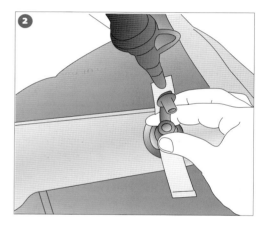

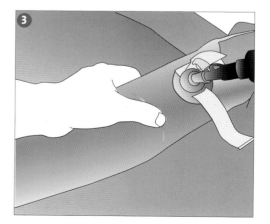

Setting up an inflatable kite wing

As you'd expect, being part of the very well-developed surfing industry with its acute sense of corporate identity, merchandise, paraphernalia and giving good value, when you buy a Storm it comes in a heavy-duty and very tasteful nylon Cordura carry bag.

Inside the bag you'll find a big pump for inflating the leading edge and battens, a control bar for flying the wing, with a depower and safety system, a quad flying line set that is appropriate for the size of wing you're buying and a full instruction manual. If, for any reason, any of this equipment is not in the bag, you should contact your dealer or Flexifoil International direct. Try to remember, as you unroll the sail for the first time, how it was rolled to leave the factory so that you can do the same when you pack it away each time. You may want to try this once at home but you're going to need to know the full procedure for when you get out on the beach, lake or river side. Take a look at the diagrams, which will help make sense of it all. Memorize and follow the step-by-step preparation instructions to the letter.

If this were the start of a boarding session, now would be the moment to stop and put on your final pieces of safety equipment — crash helmet, harness and buoyancy or flotation aid. You might want to get used to this anyway while you're learning to fly the kite as that's the way it's going to be when you come to do it for real. To begin with,

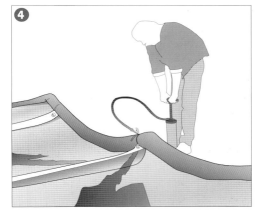

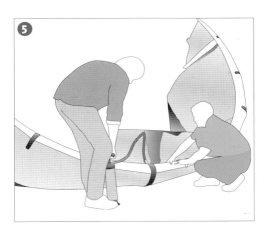

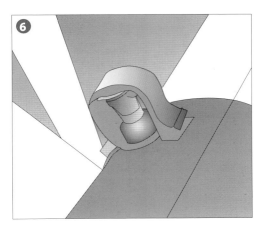

though, get used to flying the wing without your harness until you've fully mastered flying it. It's a completely different experience flying a big kite wing with your movement restricted by your wetsuit, harness and so on. Specially built kiteboarding wetsuits and harnesses are now being produced and these are designed with extra flexibility where kiteboarders need it.

The next stage will be to unwind your flying lines. Riders tend to use long lines (35 to 40 metres) in light to moderate wind and shorter lines (20 metres) in strong wind. As you will be learning in light to moderate winds, you should have a line set of 35 to 40 metres long. The lines must be the appropriate strength for the size of your wing and wind, taking into account that when you use a kite on water there is about 30 per cent more strain on the flying lines than when flying on land. This is due to the extra resistance of the water against your board and body. In fact, your lines are almost certainly made of high-quality Spectra or Dyneema with its advantages of low stretch, low weight, low diameter (in relation to nylon or polyester lines of the equivalent strength) and good slipperiness. As with a four-line ram air wing, the front lines will be thicker and stronger than the rear lines as they are the ones that carry most of the pressure and loading from the wing. They will be sleeved at each end to prevent snapping where knots are tied (Dyneema and Spectra have low melting points so friction from knots would cause the lines to cut through themselves at

the knot). This sleeving will be colour coded to help you identify the stronger and weaker lines easily.

Hydro line is a special Dyneema line sleeved along its entire length in Dyneema polypropylene. It floats and is brightly coloured (otherwise, all lines are white) so you can see it better on or in the water.

Whichever sort of flying lines you're using, unwind them fully and attach your handles or control bar as described in the kite or wing instruction manual. Always take great care to correctly separate and attach the flying lines to the correct sides of the wing or kite and the handles or control bar. Ready? I think you are.

How to launch an inflatable wing

As with the other Flexifoil kites and wings, there are two ways to launch an inflatable wing such as the Storm — assisted launch (recommended for beginners) or solo launch (recommended for more experienced flyers only). The assisted launch is advisable when you're starting out because, until you're used to the handling, there's a chance that you could get into difficulties. In fact, in big winds and with big wing sizes, it's a good idea to use the assisted launch however much experience you've got. You're going to

▸ *Weighting down your Storm*

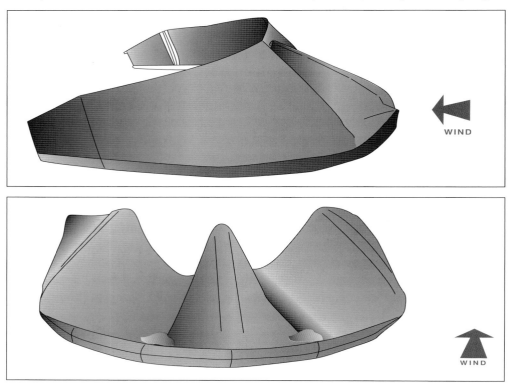

need to know how to make a solo launch, too, and this will be explained later.

- Step 1: For an assisted launch, make sure you brief your helper before you start. The positioning of the wing or flyer is the same as described below for a solo launch. Your helper should stand downwind, behind the wing set up on the ground.
- Step 2: When you're ready to launch, as you start to move backwards and pull gently on the control bar, your helper needs to hold the downwind tip of the wing up to the wind and, as it lifts up, hold the leading edge of the wing to stabilize it during this phase.
- Step 3: With the wing full of wind and ready to go, your helper holds it by the centre of the leading edge, from where they can do one of two things: on your launch signal, they release the wing, take a few steps backwards to get out of the way and let you fly the wing to safety; on your signal to abort the launch, grab the wing quickly, then turn it on it's back to depower and immobilize it again. What you must do is agree your signals beforehand and for your helper to simply release the wing at the appropriate moment, not try to throw it.
- once the wing is out of your helper's hands, you follow the normal procedure for steering the wing up to the zenith, as described next.

For the unassisted launch let's assume you're in position and so is the wing, which is on its back at about 45 degrees to the centre of

▸ *The assisted launch steps 1-3*

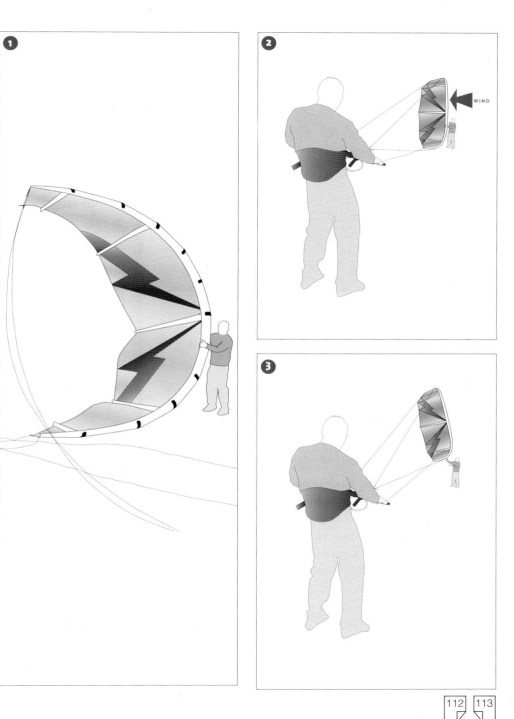

the wind window, its leading edge facing the edge of the window. Make sure you fold its upwind tip over and weight it down with sand. If you don't fold the wing tip over, there's a chance that the sand won't be removed and it may foul your launch.

- Step 1: Take a couple of paces backwards, pulling smoothly, gently and evenly on the control bar as you go. Tension will come on to the downwind tip lines, making the tip rise off the ground. As it does, you will feel pressure beginning to build in the sail.
- Step 2: Keep moving gently backwards and the downwind tip will rise further. Then, tension will come on to the upwind tip and lines, pulling it towards you. As it does, it will unfold and dump its load of sand on the ground. Hold the bar diagonally in the same plane as the wing to help maintain its position facing the edge of the wind window. You will now feel considerably more pressure on the lines as the wing fills with wind.
- Step 3: Once the wing has got rid of its sand, it will lift itself off the ground and, as long as you keep even pressure on the flying lines, fly to a 'safe' position on the edge of the wind window.
- from here you can steer it up the wind window, pulling gently on the upper tip and lines, until it reaches the zenith, above your head. Neutralize your steering to stabilize the wing there.

▶ *The unassisted launch steps 1-3*

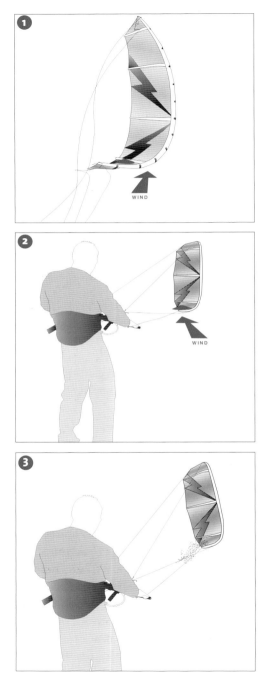

Steering the wing

With the wing stable at the zenith, this is the moment when, if you were boarding, you would hook into your harness and get your board leash fastened ready to hit the water. During your first few sessions, while you are mastering the flying controls, you are advised not to hook in. You need to know how to fly the wing confidently before adding new dimensions such as the harness.

At this stage, your only way of controlling (as in reducing) power is to move forwards or steer the wing further out of the window. It's going to be a good workout because you'll be dealing with the full power of the wing with your arms then your body, rather than the other way round. Try moving the wing backwards and forwards across the top of the wind window at first. The steering technique is very similar to that for a two-line kite, despite the fact that you have four control lines with this wing. See opposite.

- 1. Pull back gently but firmly on the right side of the control bar, at the same time pushing forwards with the left, until you see the wing start to turn to the right. As soon as it's pointing slightly to the right, neutralize your steering to let it fly in that direction. It may descend slightly as it does so.
- 2. Before it reaches the edge of the window, pull gently but firmly back on the left end of the control bar until you see the wing turn to face slightly left. Neutralize your steering to let the wing fly back across the top of the window. It will probably rise a little towards the centre of the window and

fall again as it moves slightly left. Don't forget, the wind window is curved.

- 3. Before it reaches the left edge of the window, pull back again on the right side and so on. You can stabilize the wing at the zenith by turning the wing to point straight up as you reach the centre of the window.

Once you've done that a few times, it's time to try some full loops. Even though that kind of manoeuvrability isn't often called for in kiteboarding, knowing how to do it improves your overall ability to control the wing, which is beneficial.

- 4. With the wing stable at the zenith, pull back firmly on the right tip of the control bar, pushing forwards with the left also. The wing will turn to the right and then continue to turn as long as you keep steering it that way.
- 5. Keep steering it that way and it will gradually travel through 360 degrees, down and to the right, coming round to point straight up the wind window again near the centre. Keep the steering on even when the wing is pointing straight down and accelerating hard. As it comes round towards the centre, the pull will be close to max and you will need to lean back, keeping your shoulders well back.
- 6. As the kite comes round full circle and is pointing straight up the wind window, neutralize your steering to allow it to climb up towards the zenith. At this point the wing will start to decelerate and lose pull.
- just before it reaches the zenith, pull back firmly on the left side of the control bar to

pull the wing into a left-hand loop. Keep the steering on all the way round until the wing is pointing straight up and climbing up the centre.

- at this point, your lines have returned to their untwisted state and you are ready to start the whole thing again.

Once you have mastered the right and left loops, you can fly around and explore the wind window, feeling the pull in different positions in the window. Standing on the ground, you will feel good, continuous pull doing a flat figure of eight (successive left and right loops) in the sky. Once you get out on the water, there's another kind of manoeuvre you will need to know for those occasions when you need to 'work' the wing if the wind is light for the size you're flying. It's a kind of 'S' pattern on its side, or sinusoidal shape, that you fly near the edge of the wind window to keep powering the wing up as you move it around.

- 7. With the wing stable at the zenith, pull back firmly but gently on the right end of your control bar to turn the wing to the right. Keep turning it until it is pointing downwards at 45 degrees. As it comes down the side of the wind window, it will begin to power up and accelerate.
- 8. As the wing reaches a 45-degree angle to the ground, pull back firmly on the left end of your control bar, turning the wing up at 45 degrees again (a 90-degree turn). Keep the steering on and turn the wing so that it climbs up the wind window.

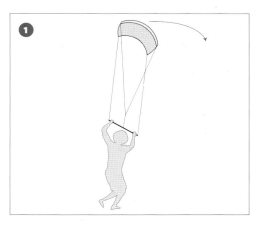

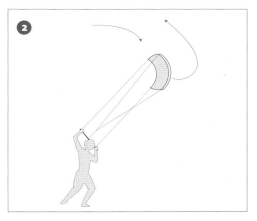

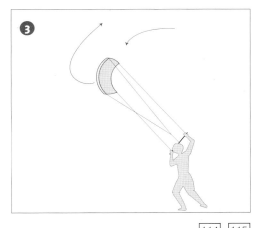

- 9. before the wing slows down and loses power, pull on the right end of your control bar again to turn the kite through 90 degrees to the right and down again, where it will once again power up and accelerate towards the ground as before.

At this point you can keep the wing moving in a continuous pattern, 'working' it up and down the edge of the wind window to try and gain power. The lower the wing comes in the sky, the more lateral pull there will be and the more you can work your board's edges.

Landing an inflatable wing

As with the launch, the landing is a potentially hazardous moment, so it should always be made with a helper. It is not actually possible to solo land and it should not be attempted.

First of all, you must have a big enough landing area that is away from other users of the site. If you are with a group of kiteboarders, you must agree where your landing and launching areas are before starting and always head for there when you want to get off your board and land the wing. You need to have your helper correctly positioned about 30 to 40 metres downwind of you (depending on your line length) at the edge of the wind window. The helper needs to approach the wing from behind, downwind, as you fly it close to the ground.

▸ *Steering the wing*

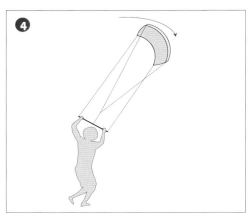

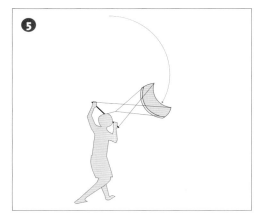

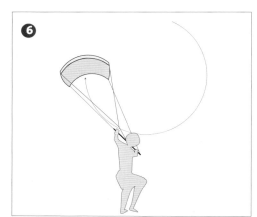

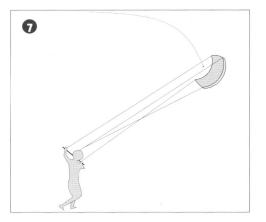

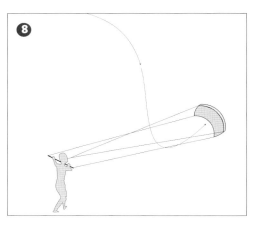

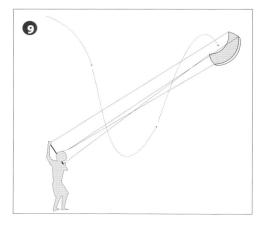

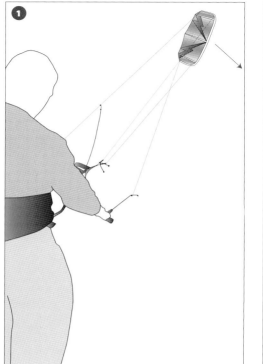

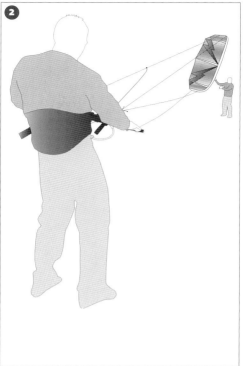

- Step 1: With the wing at the zenith, pull gently on the right end of your control bar and turn the wing to the right. Don't pull it into a full loop – steer it gently but steadily down the edge of the wind window, keeping the leading edge pointing towards the edge of the wind window, never straight down.
- as the wing approaches ground level, manoeuvre yourself on the ground so you can fly the wing close to your helper. Keep flying the wing out towards the edge of the window so there's minimum power.
- Step 2: Your helper should move to a

▲ *Landing the wing*

position where the kite can be approached from behind, downwind of it. When your helper can reach the centre of the leading edge, he or she should grab it, turn the wing on its back and be ready to 'walk' it to a safe position to immobilize it.

- you can now detach your board and safety leashes and walk the wing to a safe position. Place the wing face down, leading edge pointing into the wind, and weight the leading edge down with sand to immobilize it.

As with the launch, the landing should be made when you're not hooked on to your harness. If you start with the wing at the

zenith and fly it down the edge of the window it should have little or no power as it descends.

The depower system

Your Flexifoil Storm kiteboarding wing is fitted with a very effective power control system that is simple to operate. It's all linked to your harness and control bar and, once you start flying hooked into your harness, you will find that it's very easy to adjust to and wonder how life ever functioned normally beforehand.

Using the depower system means flying with your harness on, so make sure you have fully mastered flying the wing without the harness before you move on to this stage.

On the control bar, there are two harness loops, or strops, in the centre. These are heavy-duty vinyl-coated loops about 15 and 20 cm (6 and 8 inches) long. The longer one is attached directly to the bar. This is called the power strop and, once you hook into this, you are committed to full-on power until you unhook again. The other loop is fitted on to the end of the leader line for the wing's front lines, which passes through a special fitting mounted at the centre of the control bar. Further along this leader line, towards the line attachments, there is a 'stop' fixed in position. Once you are hooked into the short harness loop, you can regulate the power by pushing the bar away from you evenly with both hands. With the front lines fixed to your harness, this has the effect of pushing the rear lines only away, breaking the profile of the trailing edge, changing the angle of attack, spilling the wing's wind and losing power.

With skill and practice, you will be able to fine tune the power at various points of your kiteboarding activity — during jumps, for instance, to tweak some extra oomph out of what you're doing. Equally valuably, it enables you to deal with big gusts and squalls out on the water, limiting the power surge and, hopefully, giving you the breathing space you need to ride it out and wait for the power to drop again. In fact, any time you feel that the power is too much and you're hooked into your depower loop you can use it in this way.

You can take it a step further, too. If you let go of the bar altogether, it will slide along the leader line until it meets the 'stop'. This releases the rear lines and keeps the front lines pulled. What normally happens is that the kite almost completely depowers and flies itself to the edge or top of the wind window where you can recover it.

Get plenty of practice on dry land with your depower system, trying it in every conceivable circumstance, before you find yourself trying to work out how to do it out on the water.

Please be aware that if you're flying a four-line ram air wing on handles or a two-line wing on a control bar, you will not have an effective depower system. In the former scenario you will have the handles to make adjustments to the angle of attack of the wing and, if it all gets too much, a wrist

▶ *Right: Depowering the kite*

▶ *Far right: Depower system in operation*

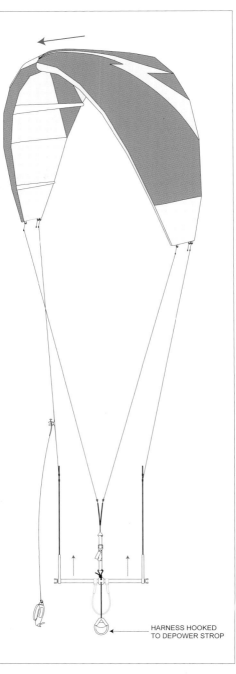

HARNESS HOOKED
TO DEPOWER STROP

leash for safety (see below). A two-line control bar has either a leash safety system or, in some cases, is fitted with a third line coming from the centre rear of the wing, attached to the centre of the bar on a leader with a stop. Letting go of the bar pulls on the third line, applying maximum brakes and depowering the wing, causing it to sink to the ground or water.

The safety system

Kiteboarding being the dangerous activity that it is, safety very quickly became an issue. Some kind of safety system was needed that would allow you to let go of the control bar or handles to totally depower the wing but stay attached to it so you could recover it afterwards. Even after the depower system was devised, riders still felt in need of some kind of ultimate get-out, especially for those moments when you're not hooked on to your depower loop. The Storm comes with exactly this kind of system and, again, it works very simply.

The safety system takes the form of a wrist leash with a Velcro fastening at one end and a loop of line at the other. The loop is attached to the end of the leader line of one of the rear lines using a lark's head knot, on the same side as the wrist to which you attach the Velcro fastening. In cases of ultimate emergency, you simply let go of the control bar, actioning the leash to pull hard on the rear line it's attached to. This pulls the

▸ *Right: Safety leash*
▸ *Far right: Powering up the kite*

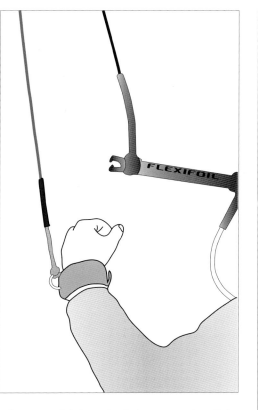

wing completely out of shape, causing it to lose all power and descend to the ground or water, depending on your location. From there, you can recover the bar on the end of its leash, sort out the wing and relaunch.

It's vitally important that you totally familiarize yourself with the safety procedure before you go out on a board. Try it in shallow water so you can practice recovering your bar and wing in water before you have to do it for real when you're out of your depth. Remember, your safety system will only work if you are unhooked from your harness. Therefore, avoid going into risky, maximum danger manoeuvres hooked in.

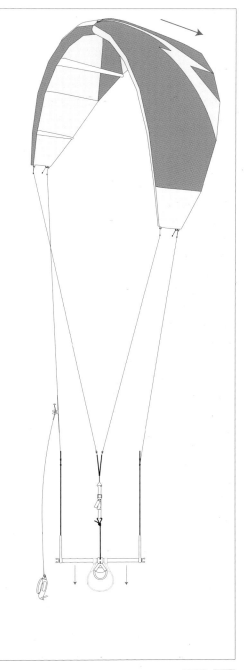

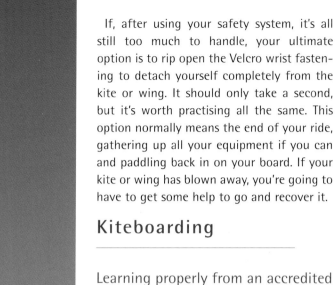

If, after using your safety system, it's all still too much to handle, your ultimate option is to rip open the Velcro wrist fastening to detach yourself completely from the kite or wing. It should only take a second, but it's worth practising all the same. This option normally means the end of your ride, gathering up all your equipment if you can and paddling back in on your board. If your kite or wing has blown away, you're going to have to get some help to go and recover it.

Kiteboarding

Learning properly from an accredited teacher or school

It goes without saying that what you're about to do is highly dangerous. Not only is there the immense power of the wing, there are the hard edges of the board, which can hurt, and then there's the small matter of the water — drowning, being lost at sea and so on. In circumstances such as these, as a complete beginner, much the best thing you can do is go and take a series of lessons at an accredited school. That way, you get the right sort of advice and training in a secure environment with rescue boats, full insurance and all the other creature comforts that make learning easier. You can test out equipment before you buy (assuming you haven't already) and see if you actually think you've got the endurance to get through the learning phase. Everybody says that as a complete beginner you've got to expect to

◀ *Freedom — a kiteboarder sets sail*

drink a lot of water during your first few sessions. Everybody also says that there's nothing like the experience of your first successful run on a kiteboard.

Whether you've come from a boarding background or a kiting background, lessons will still be a good idea as there's at least 50 per cent of the package you know little or nothing about at this stage.

'Accredited' by who exactly? Early on in the life of kiteboarding in the UK, an association was formed with the express purpose of coordinating the new sport's activities. Top of the list were safety, teaching and getting new people involved. The organization that was formed is the British Kite Surfing Association (BKSA). Not only is it the accrediting body for schools, it runs a website and information centre for kiteboarding activities in the UK. Membership costs relatively little (compared to the equipment) and, importantly, includes insurance. You might well find classes available via your local kite or windsurfing dealer, at a wind or watersports centre, marina, beach windsurfing school or other such places. Check that they are BKSA accredited before you book.

There's one worldwide body that has a similar function, instructs instructors and approves courses. It's called the International Kiteboarding Organization (IKO). The IKO is sponsored by a number of big name manufacturers, including Flexifoil, as a means of safely promoting and coordinating the sport.

A good kiteboard school will have classes for different skill levels. Be honest about

▸ *Getting ready to go*

on planing with the kite locked at the edge of the window. It's all in the feet again.

If the wind is strong enough, with a four-line set-up you can virtually 'lock' the wing in position at 45 degrees to the water and concentrate on holding your course with the board. Apparent wind comes into play again and the more you can steer the board across and slightly upwind, the faster you will be able to go.

If you want to try and get further upwind, with the water to lever against, you can bring the kite or wing further down the wind window to power up and then use heel pressure to carve the edge into the water, wedging the board and pointing it more upwind. Once you're pointing the right way, take the wing back up the edge of the window and press with your front foot on the board to straighten up again.

If the wind is on the light side for your size of wing or kite, you will need to 'work' it more using the 'S' pattern described previously. The effect of this on the board is that, as the wing descends and picks up power, it accelerates towards the edge of the window. You must then work the back side edge and steer upwind to avoid catching up with the wing, causing it to lose power and possibly collapse. You need to find a good rhythm of powering up, increasing speed, turning upwind and then gradually straightening again as the wing or kite climbs. The weaker the wind, the more exaggerated the 'S' of the kite and weave pattern of the board will need to be.

Changing direction and turning round

"Learning any skill is worthwhile as it will help you with something more complicated later on. Gybing is an outdated concept in kiteboarding now, but the skills learned will benefit wave riding later. Even on flat water, it's really good fun doing a hard carve gybe on a wakeboard and popping the board back round on the exit."

Chris Calthrop
Flexifoil-sponsored kiteboarder

We're talking about gybing. If you're using a directional board, it's an essential manoeuvre to learn. Even for those of you riding twin tips, it's still something you can use and that you really need to know. Riding a wakeboard or twin tip with full foot bindings means that gybing presents a different set of issues as it will leave you riding back side on the front side edge — that's to say, leaning forwards rather than back and flying the wing over your leading shoulder. That, though, doesn't really concern us here because what we're interested in is the standard gybe.

In one sense it's similar to the basic windsurfing gybe, which brings the rider round to ride on the other, opposite edge of the board to the one they were on before gybing, but there all similarity ends. With no fixed mast to hold on to, in kiteboarding it becomes a question of balance and timing to turn the board, step over into the foot straps on the other

side and resume planing, all the while balancing yourself against the pull of the kite. There's a scary moment when you're out of the straps and face on to the wing and then timing is very much the crucial factor. You are strongly advised to try the foot movements several times on your board on dry land, without the wing, so you are confident about that element before you try it on water.

- 1. you're planing along with good forward speed. The board is flat rather than riding on the edge. Time to unhook from your harness and get ready to move.
- 2. take your rear foot out of its strap and put it just in front of it. Flex and press with your front foot to tilt the board forwards more, pressing the rail into the water. Bend your rear knee at the same time to make the tilting smooth, firm and even.
- 3. control the tilt of the board with your free (rear) foot. Steer the wing straight up to the zenith where it will stay during the next phase. Hold the control bar or handles at arm's length and start to physically turn the board with your feet.
- 4. as the board turns, you find your body coming round to ride the back side with your back towards the wing. Keep the wing at the zenith.

Now take your front foot out of its strap and bring your rear foot up so that you're standing, feet parallel and pointing forwards along the board, just beside or behind the front foot strap.

Keeping the wing at the zenith still, quickly reverse the positions of your feet, putting what was your rear foot into the front strap

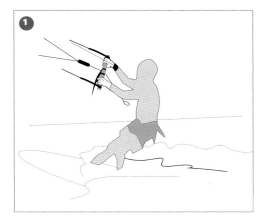

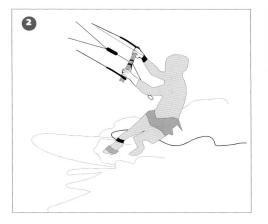

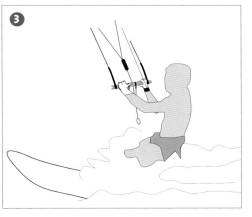

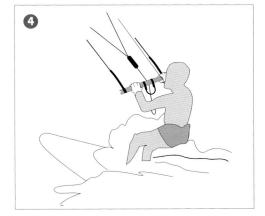

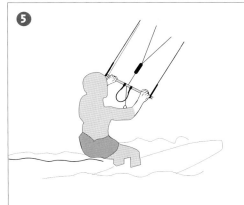

and your other foot into the rear strap.

- 5. before you've got the board through its turn, try to start the wing moving again into the power zone and towards the edge of the wind window you want to move towards. Lean back to counteract the pull and off you go again in the opposite direction.

If you can master the gybe, then, in many ways, you've got over the most difficult bit. The things to avoid if you want to have the best chance of hitting a good gybe are:

- not having enough forward speed going into the manoeuvre
- not tilting the board enough
- allowing power back into your wing too soon, resulting in a wipeout
- not getting your wing going soon enough to power up again, resulting in sinking.

It's a lot to think about and, as with previous moves, may take you many attempts to get right. To make it easier, try it all on a big-volume board with a wing that is not too powerful or big. The idea is to make it one continuous, smooth movement, turning the board quickly and getting it moving again before it has a chance to slow and sink.

You may be learning on a twin tip board, in which case no gybe is needed. However, you still need to know how to turn round. It's like on a mountainboard.

- as you're planing along, steer the wing up the edge to the top centre of the window

◀ *Changing direction 1-5*

where it will lose power and you will slow down.

- as you slow down almost to a stop, shift your weight, ready to go back the other way.
- before you feel the board sink, steer the wing to the edge you want to move towards, bracing yourself for the power coming back on.
- 'lock' the wing in position and away you go.

If you are able to start up, plane on the board, work the edges to go upwind a bit more and turn round to get back to your start point, you've got all the basic manoeuvres you need to start out in the exciting world of kiteboarding — the most exhilarating new extreme sport around.

From now on it's practice, practice, practice. It's good to go solo riding, but you will learn a lot by riding with other, more experienced riders — watching what they do, asking them how they do it. With your own growing level of skill and experience and the benefit of theirs you will progress more quickly than you would sailing alone and soon be ready for some more radical and dangerous moves.

Stopping

Hopefully you're only going to need to stop for one reason — when you want to get back to dry land. It may be that other emergencies dictate that you stop out on the wateA dead stop will sink you for sure. Even on a larger-volume directional board, the chances are you will be down in the water, although your wing should be safely positioned and you

shouldn't need to water launch it. You should be hooked on to your short harness loop and depower system.

- as you are reaching across the wind and nearing the beach, start steering the wing up the edge of the wind window to lose power and slow down.
- at the same time, start leaning back to work the rear edge and turn your board upwind.
- steer the wing to the zenith and, when the board is pointing upwind, press with your front foot to bring the board upright.
- step off the board quickly and, keeping the wing stable at the zenith with one hand, pick up your board with the other and leave the water, detach yourself from the board and follow the normal procedure for an assisted landing.

The idea is to stop close enough to dry land to be in shallow water and step off the board. If you have to execute your stop in deeper water, obviously you won't have that luxury, but your wing should be stable up at the zenith and it will give you another chance to practice your water restart. It's all a question of timing as usual. With skill and practice you'll be able to stop suddenly, but always be careful as you steer the wing up the window not to get it too far behind you or it will pull you over. Neither do you want it too powered up or you'll be heading for an unexpected jump. Stopping at exactly the right place on the edge of the beach is an acquired skill. Whatever type of board you're on, don't approach your landing spot with too much speed — always err on the side of caution.

Jumping

"You need good wind, a fast, efficient kite, a thin board ... and balls. Send it!"

Chris Calthrop
Flexifoil-sponsored kiteboarder

It's one thing checking out the great photos in kiteboarding magazines and books such as this and seeing the occasional piece of footage on television or video, but it's quite another actually witnessing a skilful rider (better still several in a big competition) hitting some big airs. As soon as you see it, you know you want to give it a go. It's incredibly impressive and the hang time seems to go on and on. With variable incidence power control a rider can even turn the power level up while in the air to extend a jump. Then there are the tricks as well. Watching the likes of Furness, Calthrop, Seales, Wharry, Trow and co. flying past, 10 metres (11 yards) above the water, upside down, is a huge attention grabber and is one of the main reasons so many people want to learn the sport.

There are three distinct phases to each jump: preparation and getting airborne, being in the air and the landing. It may take longer to learn the final element than any of the rest and you must be prepared once again for a lot of falls and drinking of water when you're not thirsty, having just learned how to ride well enough not to. No gain without pain. Even when you've learned how to do the whole thing, it won't stop there because once you prove to yourself that you can do it, you'll want to keep going for bigger and better jumps. Those big jumps mean big wipeouts. At least as a kiteboarder you've got the cushioning water to land in rather than a hard surface to slam into. Nevertheless, be careful — water can still seem very hard and hurt a great deal if you hit it at speed.

For your first attempts it will be better if you're on flat water rather than waves or a swell. Learn how to jump properly, then you can start playing trampolines with the water contours later on. As ever, you'll be wanting a smooth wind that is strong enough to get you off the water but not so strong that everything happens too fast or too hard. Try with a medium-size kite while you get used to the mechanics, technique and sensations. Remember, this is pretty much maxi danger — in the air, over water, powered by a big kite wing and not in 100 per cent control of what happens next, however good you are. It's better to be hooked on to the short harness loop and depower system during your first jumps. It allows you to control the power during the jump and makes it simple to let go of everything if you get into difficulties mid jump. Fixed into the long loop, you can't control it and will therefore have max power all through the jump. If you're riding with a two-line wing, you should unhook altogether for exactly that same safety reason. For a good jump, you need a combination of speed and good timing.

• steer the wing low down on the edge of the wind window so that you're as powered up as possible and sailing slightly upwind, pressing hard with your heels to work the edge in the water. You need a good body position to get ready to go airborne, knees bent, body flexed and braced, ready to spring.

- keep working the edge so as not to lose any speed. Start steering the wing so that it comes slightly back into the wind window, pulling very slightly with the line attached to the top wing tip.
- as you do this, try to relax some of the pressure on the board so you are less on the edge and more on the flat of the board. Keep moving the wing towards the centre and top of the wind window, pointing straight up.
- keep working on the board until the pull of the wing in the centre of the window is too much to hold. Now, spring into the air, letting the wing pull you off the water as you do so. The wing should still be in the centre of the window.
- all being well, you are now airborne and will really feel the lift effect of the wing. Enjoy every second, but keep a careful eye on the wing and make sure is stays where you put it. Don't get it moving towards the edge again too early or you'll have a very hard, fast splashdown — keep it as directly above your head as possible.
- get back into a good, braced, flexed body shape for the landing, which is coming up very soon. The wing may well be a little behind you now and it's time to get it back into meaningful action. Don't let it go too far behind you. Pull slightly on your forward hand to start bringing it forwards in the window and have a look to make sure it has started turning. Getting power back in the wing at the right moment means a softer landing.
- brace yourself for landing. Watch the water as you approach and, if you think you're going too fast with the wing pulling more than you'd like, try to place the board so it's pointing slightly downwind to lose a bit of speed. If the opposite happens and you land heavily with little power, dig your rear edge in, steer the board as upwind as possible to try and power the wing up quickly. Bend your knees on landing to absorb any impact and get yourself planing again quickly.

The trick with learning to jump is having the correct wing size — too big and you won't be able to manoeuvre it quickly enough; too small and it will be too fast. When you get it right, you really are on the way to maxing your sensations. If it's that good to watch, imagine what it must feel like up there on the board.

Don't stop there. You can learn how to control the power of your jumps to go higher or lower, master your wing control to get the best possible landings and go for bigger and better jumps. Then you can start throwing in some tricks, starting with some basic grabs perhaps, and then see where you go after that. It won't be too long I'm sure before you're hitting those big upside down numbers — some rotations perhaps ...

Back to shore

It's going to happen sooner rather than later. As usual, there's a simple step-by-step procedure — one that you definitely need to practice several times in shallow water before it happens in choppy sea further out than you care to imagine. In those circumstances, if there's no rescue boat around, it becomes not so much a question of getting started again as saving your life.

Your board will be on the end of its leash and very useful presently for getting everything back to land. For now, you need to concentrate on finding your control bar or handles and making sure that the flying lines aren't twisted around your legs or the board under the water.

- once you've found the control bar or handles, start winding in the flying lines while swimming slowly towards the wing. Wind the lines as far as just in front of the wing.
- now straighten out the wing. If it's an inflatable, the first thing to do is deflate the vertical battens using the valves, starting with the tips and working your way inwards to do the centre one last. Then, deflate the leading edge. Each time you deflate a tube, be careful not to allow any water into it. Likewise, once they're deflated, close the valves properly.
- from this point on, the procedure is the same for ram air or inflatable wings. Place the control bar on one tip and roll the wing up around the control bar. If you're rolling up a ram air, try to squeeze the air out through the vents as you roll to make a less bulky package.
- with the kite or wing in this compact form, you can put it on your board. Take your harness off so the hook doesn't cause discomfort while lying on the board, attach it to the rear strap, lie on the board and paddle back in.

Once you're back to dry land, it's time to reinflate the tubes or dry out your ram air and quickly check that the flying lines are OK before getting yourself relaunched and restarted.

It's possible to buy a kiteboarding backpack or waist pouch to wear while you're riding. Either of these would be a useful accessory to have during this exercise, because you can put the wing in the pouch or pack, attach the harness to it and your rear foot strap and paddle your board in, towing the whole lot behind you.

You can practice all this on those days when there's enough wind to fly the wing, but not to get up on the board. Make sure it's second nature to you before the issue is forced on you in less than forgiving circumstances.

Basic rules for kiteboarding safety

As mentioned, when you start playing around with the awesome power of traction wings and then add the extra mystery ingredient of water, it's a recipe for extreme fun but also for extreme danger. Putting safety first, second and third is essential because, if it ever appears that kiteboarding is unnecessarily risky, there will be calls for it to be prohibited.

Safety was the primary reason for the founding of the British Kite Surfing Association (BKSA). It quickly took on the role of educating riders and training trainers as soon as the new sport started to receive attention and attract newcomers. It has drawn up a set of basic safety guidelines that apply to riders of all skill levels, but especially beginners. They identify several basic skills a rider must have acquired in order to move successfully on to the water. These guidelines are reprinted here in full (our thanks to the BKSA for allowing us to do this).

Kiteboarding is an extreme sport and is therefore potentially dangerous to both the kitesurfer and others. The overriding need is for rider responsibility. This shouldn't put anybody off or sound too officious, but, with so many newcomers to kiteboarding, it was felt that it would be very wise to lay out a complete set of the safety guidelines.

Kitesurfing should not be attempted without appropriate instruction.
The minimum competence levels are considered to be as follows.

Level 1: kite-flying skills

- understand all aspects of safe handling of kites on land and water.
- able to launch and land (unaided) on a specified spot on land.

Level 2: basic water skills

- body surfing with kite (along and back to shore).
- water launching on to the board.

Level 3: basic kitesurfing skills

- getting on a board and travelling a distance under kite power.
- emergency stop on water — getting off the board quickly and stopping with the kite aloft.
- returning to base on land by kitesurfing, paddling or body surfing home.

General safety guidelines

- stay clear of power lines and overhead obstructions.
- never fly a kite in a thunderstorm.
- always inform the beach warden, lifeguard or coastguard where and when you will be kitesurfing (kites can look like planes crashing to the uninitiated).

Britain's beaches, airspace and ocean environment belong to everyone and must be kept safe, clean and free.

Kite contraindications

- if you cannot walk backwards when the kite is flying at minimum power (overhead), the kite is too big and/or the wind is too strong.
- never tether yourself to the kite with a closed system. Only use open, quick-release harness systems, if any.
- never attempt kitesurfing if you don't already have a good level of kite-flying experience.

Site etiquette

- do not lay kite lines across anyone's path.
- do not launch or land in crowded areas.
- always announce you are launching a kite.
- select a safe launching site.
- prevent kites from relaunching by weighting them down with sand or other ballast.
- disable unattended kites.

Water

- never kitesurf in areas congested with swimmers, boats, other craft and obstacles.

- never go out on the water without telling another person where you're going.
- always maintain a downwind safety buffer zone to allow for being pulled downwind.
- a kitesurfer must know the rules of the sea, including navigation laws, and abide by them at all times.
- instruction must be taken from an experienced kitesurfer before attempting kitesurfing for the first time.
- a kitesurfer should be fit and healthy and over 18 years of age (under 18s must provide written parental permission).
- if going offshore, kitesurf in pairs or with a rescue boat in attendance.
- never kitesurf in conditions that are too extreme for you or your equipment.

Equipment

- all manufacturers' instructions and safety guidelines must be read and followed with particular regard to the limitations of the product.
- equipment must be checked regularly for wear and tear and repaired or replaced before going on to the water.
- always use adequate safety equipment.
- be safe — wear a helmet.

Essential equipment

The full list of kiteboarding essentials depends to a large extent on where you're going to do the majority of your riding. The air and water temperature will make a huge difference, for example, to the thickness of your wetsuit and, indeed, might mean you

don't wear one at all. Suffice to say, there's an armoury of other pieces of equipment, aside from the board and wing, that you'll need to have before you can get out on the water, wherever you're planning to plane.

- **Harness:** Absolutely essential. Generally available in two styles — the belt harness and the seat harness. The former fits just around the waist and the other has a full set of crotch straps and so on. The seat version helps get the centre of pull and balance much lower, making boarding more stable.
- **Wetsuit:** Absolutely essential almost all the time. Available in different thicknesses (anywhere from 3 to 7 mm), depending on how cold it's likely to be — 3 to 5-mm ones are the most common. They also come in different leg and arm lengths, with a shorty suit in 3 mm being the kind of thing you'd need for warm water riding. Even in tropical waters, if you plan to ride all day, a shorty suit can protect you from crash landings and hypothermia. There are different men's and women's fits. Always try them on in the shop before you buy. If they won't let you, go somewhere else.
- **Flotation or buoyancy:** Absolutely essential. Some belt-style harnesses now incorporate buoyancy.
- **Crash helmet:** Absolutely essential. There's no excuse for not wearing one.
- **Board leash:** This attaches the board to your ankle or rear of your harness via a Velcro strap fastening and length (about 2 metres/2 yards) of vinyl cord. You can ride without one if you like, but you're going to

be chasing your board all over the place.
- **Safety system:** Absolutely essential. Comes as standard with most wings nowadays.
- **Large ground stake:** For keeping wings of varying sizes ready but immobilized on days of varying wind.
- **Wind meter:** Expect to pay handsomely for a hand-held meter with any accuracy.
- **Puncture repair kit:** Essential. This is like a bicycle puncture repair kit but for the inflatable tubes that are vital to your wing's functioning.
- **Basic human repair kit:** Plasters, antiseptic, bandages, sling — this is an extreme sport remember.
- **Sun cream and ultraviolet protection:** Yes, even in northern Europe. It is needed for those parts of you not covered by your suit, which will be exposed to the elements all day.
- **Sunglasses:** As above, but for your eyes.

That's what you need to get you going, but what about all those things that can happen during the day (other than a tube bursting) that you need to cover yourself for? The more you kiteboard, the more gear you're going to accumulate for doing different things and the more potential there is for hardware failure to spoil your day out. The following things can come in very handy.

- spare flying line sets in case of a damaged or broken line.
- spare control bar.
- splicing and sleeving kit for making adjustments or repairs to flying lines.
- spare fins for your board.

- spare straps or bindings.
- tool kit with spare fittings for fins and bindings.
- spare harness (an old one, perhaps).
- different types of board depending on the conditions — a larger-volume directional or twin tip for light winds and a wake- or miniboard for strong winds and flat water.
- a reserve supply of energy bars and drinks in case, as can easily happen, you stay out riding a long time and need to get emergency energy in your body once you're back on dry land.
- a waterproof watch so you can actually keep track of time instead of losing it.

Having dealt with all the important and essential items, it's worth pointing out that kiteboarding, in common with other board and surf sports, is a very style-conscious affair. Clothing manufacturers sponsor the riders up to the eyeballs, fuelling the whole thing even further. Sure, there's looking cool during the après-surf once the water action's finished, but there's a great deal of sartorial splendour out there on the water, too. Large numbers of riders seem to resent the anonymity of the standard dark neoprene wetsuit and you'll find that there are thousands of garments on the rails and shelves to choose from.

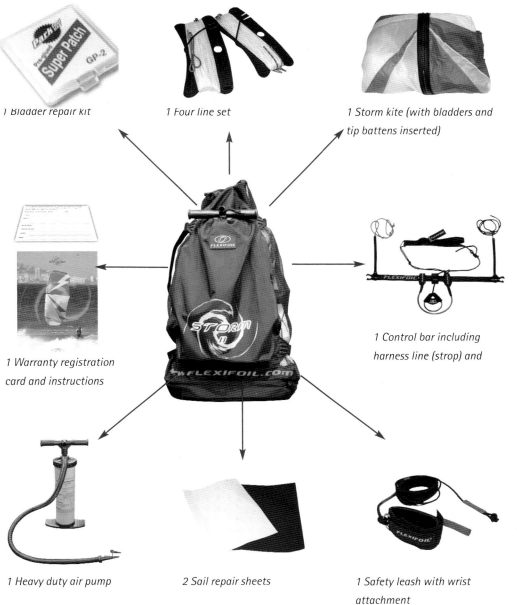

1 Bladder repair kit

1 Four line set

1 Storm kite (with bladders and tip battens inserted)

1 Warranty registration card and instructions

1 Control bar including harness line (strop) and

1 Heavy duty air pump

2 Sail repair sheets

1 Safety leash with wrist attachment

Body surfing or dragging

This is good fun and you don't even need a board or buggy. You will need a wetsuit, though, because dragging your body along through shallow water is just inviting those rocks, razor shells and other flotsam and jetsam to enter where they're not at all welcome. It's also a good way of getting used to flying and working the kites and wings while in the water.

Any stack of kites or a single big kite or wing will do the job, with any line configuration — two or four. You'll also need some kind of flotation jacket, which will help make sure your body is well up in the water if the kites or wing depower for any reason. If you're a harness user you can use that, as long as you've got a depower, safety and/or quick release system ready in case you hit a problem.

It's not complicated to do — in fact, it's much like skidding on land. You don't need to know anything too technical to get yourself going. The main thing to avoid is getting yourself out of your depth in the water until you're confident that you won't dump the kites in the water while you're body dragging.

If you were paying attention earlier on, you'll know all about flying a flat figure of eight pattern with your wing or kite slightly above the middle of the window as a means of generating constant pull on dry land. That's what you do to start skidding on the ground and, whereas you lean backwards for a good skid, you're now going to be lying on your front, letting the kites pull you along and keeping your head out of the water at the same time. Start by standing up and, once the power comes on, you plunge forwards on to your front, keeping your arms

free for steering the kites or wing. The more consistently you can keep the power on, the less water you're going to swallow.

Be aware that body surfing or dragging is not something you can or should do reaching across the wind. You do it in one direction only, downwind. This means you can only really use a side-shore wind to go along the shoreline, never getting too far from land so you are able to leave the water to get back upwind when you need to. Avoid offshore winds as these obviously could drag you out to the danger of the open sea. It's perfectly possible to cross rivers, lakes and reservoirs in this way, depending on their size, but you need to be sure you have the skill and strength to get across. You should also have some means of getting back again afterwards with your gear.

Care of
the **kite**

THE MORE POWER KITING you do, the more equipment you're going to accumulate and the more dangerous and serious its purpose often becomes. The object is to enjoy the danger while minimizing the risk, both to yourself and others. Then there are the kites and wings themselves and the flying lines that control them. It can all potentially either endanger or save your life and needs to be looked after and maintained accordingly. Apart from anything else, you've quite possibly spent a good deal of your hard-earned money buying them. Who knows, one day you might even want to start selling some of it, in which case, the better the condition it's in, the more you'll get for it.

Nothing deteriorates ripstop nylon sailcloth and other fabrics quite as efficiently as ultraviolet light from the sun. Other than salt water, that is, or sand. Put the three together and you have a pretty aggressive combination. So, while beach sites are great for wind and space, they're also a potential hazard for your kites.

Yes, it's a good idea to have different kites ready to use in case of changing wind, but bear in mind that a kite that's left out all day in bright sunlight will quickly fade and deteriorate.

If your kite gets wet with salt water, you should rinse the fabric when you get it home. Use warm (not hot) mildly soapy water, wash by hand, then rinse and dry everything thoroughly before finally packing

◀ *Keep your gauze clean for better flying*

▶ *Shake out all the sand when flying on beaches*

it away. In fact, any kite that is packed away wet from sea or rain on the flying site must be completely dried out at home. Be careful, too, of tar and oil on beach sites as these are very difficult to remove from nylon sailcloth.

Empty sand out from ram air kites as it will damage the fabric and interfere with flying. Check your kites over regularly, especially for signs of strain around the bridle or flying line attachment points and any damage to the bridle itself. Small tears and holes can be mended with clear adhesive repair tape available from your dealer. Bigger tears or holes or other general repairs should be carried out by Flexifoil, either directly or through your dealer.

Even with regular, heavy use, every weekend, a kite should last you two or three years if you look after it properly. After that time, it may well be generally used and stretched, especially if used extensively at or above its wind range limit. Then, replacement is the only option. It will certainly never fly again 'as new'.

On an inflatable wing, you should check over your inflatable tubes regularly. Punctures can be easily repaired in a similar way to a bicycle inner tube. You may need to put the inflated tube in a bowl of water to identify the leak before effecting a repair.

Check the leading edge for signs of scuffing or small nicks and tears and the line attachment points to make sure they are secure. There's a big stress point where the leading edge is joined to the sail. Check along the length of this join regularly.

▶ Top: Get all large tears repaired

▶ Bottom: Regularly check all inflatable tubes

Pay careful attention to your control lines, leader lines and any stacking lines if you're flying a stack. Worn leader lines, sleeving or connection loops must be replaced immediately. Snapping a line at 20 mph in your buggy or 5 metres off the water on your board is no joke.

Always wind your lines neatly and avoid dragging them across the ground, walking towards them as you are winding in. Check the lines for any nicks or signs of wear. The lines start their life very smooth and slippery, but may rough up with extensive use, especially if used a lot on sand. The sand grains can get in between the fibres and cause friction and wearing, interfering with flying and damaging the lines. Lines that have been used near water and sand or are simply very dirty, can be rinsed, on their winder, under running cold water. 'Tease' the lines with your fingers under the water to help wash them clean. Hang the lines somewhere to dry completely — preferably out of direct sunlight — before packing away.

A well looked after set of flying lines should last you two or three years, if not longer. Their lifetime will reduce, however, if you start adding the extra stress and loadings of buggying or kiteboarding. A set of kiteboarding lines, for instance, should be replaced every year or so.

Harnesses and harness loops are especially vulnerable to wear and tear because of the heavy load they carry. If you're using a harness, check it over regularly for signs of wear, especially round the fastenings and the

▸ *Check all moving parts on your buggy*

hook. Unexpected harness failure could cause a real problem.

Crash helmets — particularly any that have actually taken a few direct knocks — should also be regularly replaced as they become ineffective once damaged.

Buggies are made from stainless steel, making them virtually maintenance-free. Nevertheless, if your buggy is muddy or has been in salt water conditions, you are well advised to hose it down thoroughly. You can clean the seat by hand, washing it with warm soapy water, then drying it out thoroughly before packing it away.

Inspect the frame for damage or cracks periodically, too. Don't attempt any repairs yourself, though — consult your dealer or Flexifoil International.

The wheel bearings will wear with use. This is unavoidable. They are made of high-tensile, rather than stainless, steel. There are ways of prolonging their life with regular maintenance. Here's what you do.

- remove the wheel bolts occasionally and clean them.
- wash the wheels down, too, with cold water and dry them, then spray with a Teflon-type lubricant (of the kind used to lubricate bike chains).
- check the plastic hub for damage or cracks and replace if necessary.
- the bearings themselves should be replaced when worn. You can tell when this is if they are reluctant to spin freely, even when lubricated, or there is sideways movement.
- the same goes for the front fork bushes, which are made from tough nylon. You

Where
to go

8

THERE ARE LITERALLY thousands of good power kiting spots to visit on the thousands of miles of British coastline, both on and off the beaten track. For pure recreational flying, almost any good, open site that conforms to all the safety guidelines explained at the beginning of the book will do. For the more serious stuff, obviously other criteria — notably that of having the maximum amount of space and, for kiteboarding, that there is water — will apply.

Once you start getting into buggying or boarding, you will find you're much better off heading for one of the recognized sites where you might well find other drivers around — after all, kiting is a social thing. If you really want to get out on your own, 'on safari', why not join the UK's Power Kite Sports Federation (PKSF), which has a comprehensive list of approved sites for kite buggying or boarding for you to choose from and a 'season' of organized events. You can either tag along or go to one of the other sites when they're all at an event somewhere else.

If anything, there's a bit more freedom with kiteboarding. Buggies really need that hard, flat sand to run well; kiteboarders can launch from almost any type of beach. Saying that, restrictions do apply and, once again, you should consider joining the PKSF, which has a kiteboarding section called the British Kite Surfing Association (BKSA). It has an excellent website you can consult that lists literally hundreds of sites all around the UK, with guidance as to where kiteboarding

The Flexifoil team training in South Africa

is and isn't practical or encouraged, schools, safety advice and so on.

Wherever you're thinking of going, always check if local restrictions apply. In some cases you need only drive another five minutes to find restriction- and hassle-free facilities, as seems to be the case in West (restricted) and East (no restrictions) Wittering on the Sussex coast. In many places, there are seasonal restrictions linked to holiday periods when the beaches and water are simply too busy to use. Contact details for the BKSA and International Kiteboarding Organization (IKO) are in the following section. The IKO is an organization that instructs and coordinates the instruction of kiteboard instructors for inflatable wings worldwide. As such, it is a great resource of information regarding where to find kiteboarding schools around the world. (Contact details for the PKSF, BKSA and IKO are all under the heading Clubs and associations later in this chapter.)

Many dealers and retailers offer individual after-sales classes or formally structured courses that you're strongly advised to take them up on. Wherever you find a dealer, you'll find their customers somewhere nearby who will already know the best places to go and how to do it. Why not think about a weekend or week-long course at one of the power kite centres in the UK? An intensive course is the best way to learn and it's great fun to go away for the weekend with a group of like-minded people for some intensive amusement and hands-on extreme sport action.

There are dozens of kiteboarding schools to choose from now, many linked to windsurfing

and other water and extreme sports centres, equipped with rescue craft and so on. You'll now find kites and wings in many surfing shops and boards and other kiteboarding equipment in many kite shops, many of which, as mentioned, offer tuition. Also, big organizations, such as Club Med, and countless smaller companies are offering kiteboarding course holidays in various locations around the world. Always check that a school is IKO/BKSA approved before booking.

It's a bit different for buggying. There are fewer recognized centres and schools, but probably more informal tuition is available. Saying that, there are a few dedicated full-time power kite centres in the UK where you can learn a range of power kiting activities — everything from flying your first Flexifoil to getting up on a kiteboard.

If the UK is blessed with power kiting sites, so too are many other places around the world. Anywhere with good, big, empty beaches, shallow 'lagoon' water and regular good-strength winds is ideal. Lots of exotic warm water island locations that are big for windsurfing are already well established on the kiteboarding circuit, so you could do worse than start with a trip to Hawaii, or Maui — the very nerve centre of all things surf. Closer to home, the Canary Islands offer great winter warmth and excellent wind and beaches and France is the biggest European market for wind and water sports. If you really want to go exotic, though, why not try New Caledonia in the south Pacific, the Madeleine Islands in Canada, the Dominican Republic, Martinique or Guadeloupe in the Caribbean, the Greek island of Paros, Tarifa in Spain, Australia, New Zealand, Hood River or The Gorge in America, Copacabana, Rio de Janeiro, Madagascar, Egypt, South Africa ... ? Many locations now have fully equipped kiteboarding schools and/or a well-established primary location, plus good information regarding where else you can explore in the vicinity.

Inside the UK, you will find power kiters all over the place and events of various descriptions. There are some well-established sites where you'll almost always find people out either simply flying their power kites or getting into some more serious traction action. In many ways they're obvious. The whole of the south west of England (Devon and Cornwall) and south Wales, for example, are well-recognized locations for wind and water sports.

Clubs, societies and associations

There are dozens of groups, clubs and associations you can join — some local, some national and one or two international.

For the clubphobic among you, let's just go over some of the benefits you might find if you join one. Although power kiting in all its forms is growing in popularity at a phenomenal rate, individually, kiteboarding and kite buggying are still minority sports and it's helpful to have information resources at your disposal. Joining a group or association means you have access to information of all sorts that can save you learning time and raise your fun levels, help you meet like-minded individuals and find out where are

the best places to go. Almost all offer insurance cover, which is a very important consideration, and may well have negotiated a bulk discount with favourable rates and very good cover — something you might find much more difficult to match or find at all on your own.

As this book went to print, the UK power kiting scene had recently come up with a plan and structure to bring together all the various power kiting disciplines under one umbrella organization. For serious and recreational traction action freaks in the UK, this means there is now somebody looking after your interests at both a practical level (teaching, insurance, event organization, databases and so on) and regarding future development, recognition and funding to develop the respective sports nationally and regionally.

The Power Kite Sports Federation (PKSF) really does cover everything from flying your first Flexifoil 6' Stacker to hitting those big airs on your wakeboard and Flexifoil Storm. The PKSF combines the functions of all the various power kite sports' bodies in the UK, giving them one voice and more clout — a bit like building a big stack out of several individual kites. It offers combined insurance policies for all types of power kite activities, organizes and sanctions events, coordinates teaching and provides an important information resource for all power kite people. In fact, it gives recreational flyers a voice for the first time — previously only the more extreme sports were represented.

You can contact the PKSF via the existing individual bodies that make up the new group — at least until new, permanent contact details are available, which they were not at publication time (spring 2002)

Useful contacts

British Buggy Club (BBC)
PO Box 4015
Smethwick
Warley
West Midlands B67 6HJ
UK
e-mail: info@buggy.demon.co.uk
Website: www.buggy.demon.co.uk

Para Kart Association (PKA)
www.pka.org.uk

British Kite Surfing Association (BKSA)
The BKSA has no permanent office or address in an effort to keep its costs to a minimum. All its functions (membership, information and son on) are run through its excellent website and this is the primary means of contact.
www.kitesurfing.org

International Kiteboarding Organization (IKO)
Contact the IKO if you want to know about international information and the whereabouts of approved inflatable kite schools.
www.ikorg.com

Magazines, publications and videos

There are two English-language, full-colour kiteboarding magazines available in the UK and others abroad. *Kitesurf* and *Kitesurf UK*.

The first is an English-language title from French publisher Custom Publishing (the French have strong claims as the inventors of kiteboarding) and the second is published by UK publisher Arcwind. Both are widely available in specialist shops, but you may well need to place a special customer order to get them in your local corner shop.

Both titles cover kiteboarding events, tips, advice, board, wing and other equipment tests and pages and pages of colour photos from all around the world that will have you really drooling — all blue lagoons, tropical sun and deserted, palm-fringed, white sand beaches. Just the thing to keep your spirits up on those grim, grey, thick wetsuit northern hemisphere winter days.

Kitesurf also carries regular buggy event news and other kite traction sports, such as kite snow (kites on skis and mountainboards).

Kiteboarder Magazine is published in America and the content is similar to the two European magazines.

As for video, kiteboarding being such a very visual thing, there are now countless videos available crammed full of great action shots, some from competition, others simply for the hell of it. And there are quite a few teaching videos too. All in all there are far too many to list here but a quick visit to your local kite or surf dealer is sure to be rewarded with a good selection to choose from. Flexifoil themselves currently have two pure entertainment power kite video titles available : 'Power Trip', a 20 minute showcase of all sorts of power kiting nonsense with the Flexifoil crew all going ape crazy bonkers in Senegal, and 'Airheads', a 45 minute blast from Maui featuring not just the Flexi boys but a large number of the world's other top riders who are based there and some superb kiteboarding action.

One excellent instruction video well worth checking out is a made-in-the-USA, or rather Hawaii, package called 'The Boost'. It's a double cassette teaching video, with tape one dedicated to all the basic starting up stuff and tape two going on to look at more complex manoeuvres and tricks. In fact there are various manufacturers' videos out there as well and at least one instruction video would be a sound investment and sensible back up to have for when school is out and it's time to get out on your own.

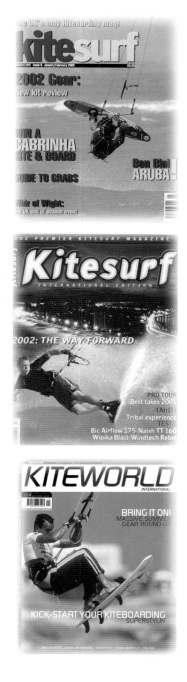

Dealer List

If you're reading this and expecting to find a long list of names, addresses and telephone numbers for your nearest stockist then look no further. Because there isn't one. It wouldn't be possible to print them all and it wouldn't be fair to leave any out.

Even just on a UK basis the number of Flexifoil stockists is enormous and, while some of them might not carry all the really serious buggy and boarding equipment, it would be unfair just to list the main dealers. Every one of them, even the little ones, have helped to make Flexifoil what it is today, one of the biggest names in world wide power kiting circles.

There are obvious places to look for Flexifoil products, kite, surf and windsurf shops being the places to start. But you'll also find racks of Flexifoil kites and other accessories in many enlightened extreme sports, outdoor pursuits, roller blade, juggling and toyshops. These in-store displays carry a loop tape power kiting video so you can enjoy some TV thrills and spills while you make your selection. The easiest way to find the nearest appropriate kind of store for you is to contact Flexifoil International direct who will be happy to put you in touch. To save you the embarrassment of a polite 'no' on the phone, Flexifoil do not sell direct to the public at fantastically reduced 'factory' prices, you must use their established dealer network. To find you nearest stockist make sure you visit Flexifoils website:
www.flexifoil.com
or contact:

Flexifoil International
27 Regal Drive
Soham
Ely
Cambridgeshire CB7 5 BE
Tel : 01353 723131
Fax : 01353 722311
Email : info@flexifoil.co.uk
www.flexifoil.com

As much as they are in demand in the UK, Flexifoil kites and traction equipment are well known and similarly available in countries all over the world including: United States, Canada, South Africa, Australia, New Zealand, Germany, France, Spain, Holland, Italy, Belgium, Norway, Sweden, Finland, Austria, Denmark Switzerland, Republic of Ireland, Mexico, Brazil, Chile, Cyprus, Bahrain. Again, for full information, contact Flexifoil direct.

Index

Page numbers in italics refer to illustrations.